PHOTOGRAPHY YEAR BOOK 1984

INTERNATIONALES JAHRBUCH DER FOTOGRAFIE 1984

CLOSEST TO PERFECTION.

Acknowledged worldwide for precision, optical perfection and total reliability, the Leitz reputation extends beyond the acclaimed Leica cameras, lenses and quality photographic accessories to Focomat enlargers, Pradovit projectors and Trinovid binoculars.
Visit an appointed Leica specialist near you and see the world's finest.

Leitz means precision worldwide.

E Leitz (Instruments) Ltd., 48 Park Street, Luton, Beds. LU1 3HP. Telephone No. 0582 413811.

PHOTOGRAPHY YEAR BOOK 1984

Edited by Peter Wilkinson Hon. FRPS

ARCO PUBLISHING, INC.
NEW YORK

© Fountain Press Ltd, 1983

Published 1984 by Arco Publishing, Inc
215 Park Avenue South, New York, N.Y.10003

ISBN 0 668 06052 2

Typeset by M & G Studios Limited

Origination by Tenreck Ltd/Thames Colour Scanning Ltd.

Printed and bound by Graficromo S.A., Cordoba, Spain.

CONTENTS   INHALT

THE NIKON FE2 PUTS AN END TO TRIAL AND ERROR.

STANDARD SLR WITHOUT FLASH. **STANDARD SLR WITH FLASH.** **NIKON FE2 WITH FLASH.**

Compare the pictures above, shot with three different SLRs at a 1/250 sec. shutter speed.

Only the FE2 delivered a complete result. Because the FE2 is the only SLR with a 1/250 sec. flash synchronisation speed. That means it can freeze the subject, fully illuminate the bike and rider, and resolve even the most minute detail, all perfectly exposed thanks to the FE2's TTL flash metering.

Quite a contrast to the other two pictures which were taken with standard SLRs. The picture on the left, taken without flash, captured the moment but no detail. While the centre picture, shot with flash,

clearly demonstrates the limitations of the lower synch. speeds of most leading SLRs.

There are many other ways we've developed the FE2 based upon the highly acclaimed specifications of the Nikon FE.

For example, the FE2 boasts lightweight titanium shutter blinds which give a top speed of 1/4000 sec.

There are three new interchangeable brighter focusing screens. And you'll appreciate the convenience of an indication of exposure compensation in the viewfinder.

So why be caught out? Put your trust in the camera that sets a standard in its class.

TRUST
Nikon

THE NIKON FE2.
THE FASTEST SLR IN THE WORLD.

NIKON UK LIMITED, 20 FULHAM BROADWAY, LONDON SW6 1BA. TEL: 01-381 1551

The Photographers/Die Fotografen

ILFORD XP1: ILFORD FP4:
ILFORD HP5: ILFOSPEED:
MULTIGRADE: ILFOBROM:
GALERIE: CIBACHROME II:
MICROPHEN: BROMOPHEN:
HYPAM:

ILFORD

PERFECT PICTURES-
WITH A LITTLE HELP
FROM YOUR FRIENDS.

Introduction by The Editor

Sitting writing these notes looking out over Las Vegas from my hotel window, having just spent four days at the Photo Marketing Association exhibition, I wonder what effect the new products seen at the Show will have on practical photography and the material submitted for future Year Books.

Thinking back to the same exhibition last year, one remembers the overwhelming impact that Kodak had with the introduction of their disc camera. I do not recall any pictures submitted this year that were taken with this camera. There is, to my mind, no reason why it cannot be exploited for serious picture making. Charles Weckler of New York had some really imaginative and moody colour prints published in the April 1982 *Popular Photography* magazine, the negatives of which were taken with a 110 camera, the grain produced by using 400 ASA film contributed greatly to the feeling of the pictures. Perhaps the publisher or Kodak should award a prize to the first photographer to have a "disc" picture published in the Year Book!

A range of auto focus 35mm compact cameras also appeared a year ago and pictures taken with such cameras were submitted this year, one author claiming that it would have been almost impossible to have taken a certain picture but for the speed of the auto focus lens. A year ago single lens reflex cameras with top speeds of 1/4000th were shown, as were intelligently programmed and auto focus or focus aided S.L.Rs. These improvements have undoubtedly had an impact on current photography and some results are seen in this year's book.

Filters of almost every shape and size with the ability to distort everything from colour to definition have been very much on display at both years' shows. It seems to me that on one hand we have the lens and film manufacturers spending vast sums to improve definition and colour rendering, and other manufacturers producing products to do just the opposite! Used intelligently, certainly these modern filters have their place in creative photography. Unfortunately, many examples submitted for possible inclusion in this year's book were just too gimmicky to warrant acceptance.

I think that the new products seen at this year's show will have a greater impact on the 1985 Year Book. I have just photographed the lights of Las Vegas with a 35–200mm zoom lens using 1000 ASA colour film and a fully programmed camera, none of which were available a year ago. Certainly in many cases one can now really concentrate on the picture and let the mechanics take care of themselves. Let us hope that such improvements will encourage us to use our creative imagination to the full.

I have been asked on numerous occasions if I have enjoyed the putting of this edition of the Year Book together and the answer is a definite yes. To me photography has always been magic and I get enormous pleasure from looking at photographs, and there were certainly plenty to look at with this year's entries.

What of the standard? By and large it was quite impressive. I was pleasantly surprised by the high standard of the colour work submitted and, in fact, it was decided in the light of so much excellent colour material to increase the number of colour pages by 16 in this year's annual.

The initial selection of pictures for the Year Book is very similar to selecting pictures for a major exhibition and of course presented the same problems. Did I, as Editor or Adjudicator, select a) pictures that I liked, or b) select pictures that I thought viewers of the book would like, or c) select pictures that I thought the viewers should see. In the end I almost ruled out pictures which fell into the categories b) and c). I do not think that a publication such as the *Photography Year Book* should be a vehicle for high-lighting national or international social injustices, nor the horrific events of the world; our newspapers and television cover these daily. One exception perhaps is the photograph of the Afghanistan orphan by Mike Hollist of the *Daily Mail*; the pathos in the little lad's face must pull the heart strings of any viewer. Over forty years ago I saw two pictures which affected my whole life because they made me aware that there was a lot more to photography than just snap-shots. The first was one of a series on the Bronte country by Bill Brandt published in *Picture Post,* and the second was of apprehensive children taking cover in a trench from German aircraft whilst hop picking in Kent. It was taken by John Topham and published in the *Daily Mail* in the very early days of the war and the picture of the Afghanistan orphan made the same deep impression.

In compiling the book, I first went through all the pictures (monochrome and colour) submitted, and divided them into three categories, a) for pictures which I definitely felt should be included, b) for pictures which I would like to include if possible, and c) which would be included if it would help with the layout. I then sub-divided these pictures into about eight categories, i.e. landscape, portraiture, pattern etc. When it came to making the final layout, due to duplication of subject matter, unsuitable format etc., it became necessary to drop a few of the a) pictures and substitute a few b) and c) to achieve a satisfactory balance. Unfortunately, this meant a small number of excellent pictures had to be omitted and, with the author's permission, some of these will be held over for possible inclusion in next year's edition.

I made no limit on the number of pictures included from any one photographer nor was I influenced by the country of origin; in fact no reference to the back of the print was made during the selection and layout.

Did the entry make me aware of any photographic trends? First, I was most impressed by the high standard of work originating in Eastern Europe. In fact the publisher and I visited Germany to ensure that we would receive a good selection of pictures from Eastern Bloc countries. These pictures showed skill and imagination in photographing fairly ordinary subjects, and the photographers from these countries seem to photograph everything from births to deaths with equal enthusiasm. Secondly, there is a greater tendency for photographers generally to take more trouble in presenting their pictures, and many of the successful prints submitted had a photographically printed edge or border. Unfortunately, for layout purposes in some cases this had to be removed.

It seems that the style of the last fifteen years or so of bleeding pictures to the edge of the printing paper may well be in for a radical change.

Thirdly, there is still a strong tendency to produce harsh or contrasting pictures with obvious grain. This technique certainly creates impact and is very suitable for certain subjects. However, in a number of pictures submitted this technique was used when it was quite incompatible with the subject matter.

To conclude, I would like to thank everyone who took the trouble to submit material for possible inclusion in the 1984 *Photography Year Book.* My congratulations to those who were accepted, my condolences to those who failed, and a very sincere request to the successful, unsuccessful and to everyone who thinks they may have suitable material to please submit for the 1985 edition.

Einführung des Redakteurs

Nach vier Tagen auf der "Photo Marketing Association" Ausstellung in Las Vegas frage ich mich beim Aufschreiben dieser Worte in meinem Hotelzimmer, während meine Blicke über die Stadt wandern, was für eine Wirkung die neuen Produkte, die ich auf der Ausstellung gesehen habe, wohl auf die fotografische Praxis und auf das Material für zukünftige Jahrbücher haben werden.

Im Rückblick auf die gleiche Ausstellung im vergangenen Jahr kann ich mich noch gut an den überwältigenden Eindruck erinnern, den Kodak mit der neuen Scheibenkamera machte. Und doch sind meines Wissens in diesem Jahr keine Bilder eingeschickt worden, die mit diesem Format aufgenommen wurden. Es besteht meiner Ansicht nach kein Grund dafür, warum dieses Format nicht auch für ernstgemeinte Aufnahmen verwendet werden kann. In der Zeitschrift "Popular Photography" erschienen in der Ausgabe April 82 einige ideenreiche und stimmungsvolle Farbfotos von Charles Weckler aus New York, die er mit einer 110 Kamera unter Verwendung eines 400 ASA Filmes aufgenommen hatte, wobei die in den Bildern festgehaltene Stimmung wesentlich durch die mit diesem Film erzielte Körnung bestimmt wurde. Vielleicht sollte der Verleger oder Kodak einen Preis ausschreiben für denjenigen, der als erster eine "Scheiben"–Aufnahme im Jahrbuch hat.

Vor einem Jahr erschienen ferner eine Reihe von 35 mm Kompakt-Kameras mit automatischer Scharfeinstellung. Mit derartigen Kameras aufgenommene Bilder wurden uns in diesem Jahr eingeschickt, wobei ein Fotograf bei einer Aufnahme kommentierte, daß sie ohne das Auto-Fokus-Objektiv praktisch nicht möglich gewesen wäre. Vor einem Jahr erschienen auch einäugige Spiegelreflexkameras mit Belichtungszeiten von 1/4000stel, sowie intelligent programmierte und Auto-Fokus- bzw. Auto-Fokus-unterstützte S.R.C.s. Diese Fortschritte spiegeln sich zweifellos in der gegenwärtigen Fotografie wider, wie Sie auch im diesjährigen Jahrbuch nachschlagen können.

Filter in allen möglichen Formen und Größen, die von der Farbe bis zur Schärfe alles verzerren können, standen sowohl auf der vorjährigen wie auch der diesjährigen Ausstellung im Vordergrund. Es scheint mir etwas widersinnig, daß auf der einen Seite Linsen- und Filmhersteller große Summen ausgeben, um Bildschärfe und Farbwiedergabe zu verbessern, während auf der anderen Seite Produkte hergestellt werden, die genau das Gegenteil bewirken! Leider waren viele für das diesjährige Jahrbuch eingeschickte Aufnahmen zu verfremdet, um angenommen zu werden.

Ich glaube, daß die auf der diesjährigen Ausstellung gezeigten neuen Produkte sich erst nachhaltig auf das 1985er Jahrbuch auswirken werden. Die Lichter von Las Vegas habe ich gerade mit einer 35–200 mm Zoomlinse unter Verwendung eines 1000 ASA Farbfilmes und einer vollständig programmierten Kamera fotografiert – Dinge, die mir vor einem Jahr noch nicht zur Verfügung standen. In vielen Fällen kann man sich jetzt rein auf das Bild konzentrieren und den Mechanismus sich selbst überlassen. Wir wollen hoffen, daß derartige Verbesserungen dazu führen, unsere kreativen Fähigkeiten voll zur Geltung zu bringen.

Ich bin bei zahlreichen Gelegenheiten gefragt worden, ob es mir Spaß gemacht habe, die vorliegende Ausgabe zusammenzustellen: die Antwort ist ein nachdrückliches Ja. Für mich ist und bleibt Fotografie etwas Zauberhaftes; die Betrachtung fotografischer Aufnahmen macht mir große Freude, und dazu hatte ich bei der Arbeit an dieser Ausgabe denn auch reichlich Gelegenheit.

Was das Niveau betrifft, so ist es im Großen und Ganzen sehr beeindruckend. Ich war angenehm überrascht von der hohen Qualität der eingeschickten Farbaufnahmen. Es waren so viele ausgezeichnete Fotos darunter, daß beschlossen wurde, das diesjährige Buch um 16 weitere Farbseiten zu bereichern.

Bei der Auswahl der Bilder für das Jahrbuch wird ähnlich wie bei der Auswahl von Bildern für eine große Ausstellung verfahren, wobei natürlich die gleichen Probleme auftraten. Sollte ich, als Herausgeber oder Schiedsrichter, a) auswählen, was mir gefällt, oder b) auswählen, was meiner Ansicht nach dem Betrachter gefallen wird, oder c) was meiner Ansicht nach der Betrachter sehen sollte. Zum Schluß entschied ich mich dafür, unter Kategorie b) und c) fallende Bilder fast vollkommen außer Acht zu lassen. Ich vertrete nicht die Meinung, daß eine Veröffentlichung wie z.B. ein fotografisches Jahrbuch dazu benutzt werden sollte, nationale oder internationale soziale Mißverhältnisse oder Schreckensereignisse der Welt aufzuzeigen; derartige Dinge sieht man in den Zeitungen und im Fernsehen. Als Ausnahme mag die Aufnahme des afghanischen Waisenknaben von Mike Hollist vom Daily Mail gelten; das Pathos auf den Zügen dieses kleinen Jungen muß jedem Betrachter ans Herz greifen. Vor mehr als vierzig Jahren sah ich zwei Bilder, die mein ganzes Leben beeinflußten, weil mir an diesen Bildern klar wurde, daß Fotografieren eine ganze Menge mehr als Schnappschüsse machen bedeutet. Das erste Bild stammte aus einer Serie von Bronte-Landschaften mit Bill Brandt, die in der Zeitschrift "Picture Post" erschienen, das zweite betraf verwaiste Kinder, die beim Hopfenpflücken in Kent in einem Schützengraben vor einem deutschen Fliegerangriff Schutz suchen. Das Bild wurde im Daily Mail in den allerersten Kriegstagen veröffentlicht. Den gleichen tiefen Eindruck rief das Bild das afghanischen Waisenkuaben hervor.

Bei der Zusammenstellung des Buches ging ich zunächst sämtliche eingeschickten Bilder, Schwarzweiß- wie Farbaufnahmen, durch, und ordnete sie nach drei Gesichtspunkten, d.h. a) nach Bildern, die meiner Meinung nach unter allen Umständen veöffentlicht werden sollten, b) nach Bildern, die ich nach Möglichkeit gern veröffentlichen wollte und c) nach Bildern, die mit einbezogen werden sollten, sofern sie für die Anordnung von Vorteil wären. Daraufhin teilte ich diese Bilder in ca. acht Kategorien ein, d.h. Landschaft, Porträtaufnahmen, Muster usw. Bei der endgültigen Anordnung zeigte sich dann, daß es aus verschiedenen Gründen, wie z.B. Verdoppelung des Aufnahmegegenstandes, ungeeignetes Format usw. notwendig war, einige der a) Bilder fallen zu lassen und ein paar b) und c) Bilder einzubeziehen, um das richtige Gleichgewicht zu erzielen. Leider bedeutete das, daß einige ausgezeichnete Aufnahmen weglassen werden mußten, die aber, soweit der Autor einverstanden ist, z.T. für nächstes Jahr vorgemerkt werden.

Ich habe es unterlassen, die veröffentlichten Aufnahmen eines einzelnen Fotografen auf eine bestimmte Anzahl zu begrenzen oder mich vom Ursprungsland beeinflussen zu lassen. Bei der Auswahl und bei der Gestaltung wurde auf die Rückseite des Bildes überhaupt kein Bezug genommen.

Und nun zu den Trenden, die mir aufgefallen sind. Zunächst möchte ich sagen, daß ich von der Qualität der aus Osteuropa eingeschickten Aufnahmen sehr beeindruckt war; ich war übrigens persönlich zusammen mit dem Verleger in Deutschland um sicherzustellen, daß uns die Ostblockländer eine gute Auswahl von Bildern zuschickten. Aus diesen Bildern – die meist ganz gewöhnliche Themen behandelten – sprach Geschick und Phantasie. Die Fotografen dieser Länder fotografieren fast alles – von der Geburt bis zum Tode – mit der gleichen Begeisterung. Zweitens scheint mir, daß die Tendenz jetzt dahin geht, mehr Wert auf die Präsentation zu legen, denn viele eingeschickte Abzüge waren mit einer photografischen Umrandung bzw. Kante versehen, die nur in einigen Fällen bei der Gestaltung weggelassen werden mußte.

Es hat den Anschein, daß der Stil der vergangenen 15 Jahre, das Bild bis an die Kante des Papieres zu ziehen, eine radikale Veränderung durchmacht.

Drittens besteht weiterhin die starke Tendenz, bei Bildern mit starkem Kontrast die Körnung sichtbar zu machen. Aber obschon dieses Verfahren sehr wirkungsvoll und auch für bestimmte Themen geeignet ist, waren eine Anzahl von Bildern dieser Art eingeschickt worden, wo es überhaupt nicht am Platze war und auch gar nicht zum Thema paßte.

Abschließend möchte ich allen denen meinen Dank aussprechen, die uns Material zur Veröffentlichung im Jahrbuch 1984 zugeschickt haben. Ich gratuliere denen, die es geschafft haben und bedaure diejenigen, die abgewiesen wurden, und bitte alle: die Glücklichen und Unglücklichen sowie jeden, der etwas in seinen Augen Veröffentlichungswürdiges herausgebracht hat, seine Arbeit für die Zusammenstellung der 1985er Ausgabe einzuschicken.

Introducción Por el Editor

Mientras escribo estas notas, sentado y mirando a Las Vegas desde la ventana de mi hotel, después de pasar cuatro días en la Photo Marketing Association Exhibition, me pregunto el efecto que tendrán los nuevos productos mostrados en la Feria sobre la fotografía práctica y el material presentado para futuros anuarios.

Pensando en la misma exposición del año pasado, recuerdo el impresionante impacto que tuvo Kodak con la introducción de su cámara de disco. No recuerdo haber visto ninguna fotografía de las presentadas este año que haya sido tomada en tal formato. Yo creo que no existe razón por la que no se pueda explotar este sistema en la práctica de fotografía en serio. Charles Weckler, de Nueva York, presentó algunas fotos en color realmente caprichosas y repletas de imaginación publicadas en la revista Popular Photography en Abril de 1982, cuyos negativos habían sido tomados con una cámara 110, y el acabado logrado con película ASA 400 contribuyó enormemente a la expresión real de las fotografías. Quizás el editor, o Kodak, debiera otorgar un premio al primer fotógrafo que tenga una foto con cámara de disco incluida en el Anuario de la Fotografía.

El año pasado también apareció una serie de cámaras compactas de enfoque automático de 35 mm. Las fotos tomadas con dichas cámaras fueron presentadas este año, y uno de los autores afirma que le hubiera sido prácticamente imposible tomar cierta foto de no ser por la velocidad de la lente de enfoque automático. En 1982 se expusieron cámaras reflex monoobjetivo con velocidades de hasta 1/4000seg., así como cámaras inteligentemente programadas de enfoque automático o asistido. Dichas mejoras, no cabe duda, han tenido su repercusión en la fotografía actual, y en el Anuario de este año se pueden apreciar algunos de los resultados.

En las exposiciones de ambos años se han visto muchos filtros de diversos tamaños y dimensiones, capaces de distorcionar todo – desde color a definición. A mi parecer, por una parte tenemos a los fabricantes de lentes y de películas, invirtiendo una fortuna para mejorar la definición y el color, mientras que otros fabricantes producen material que tiene exactamente el efecto contrario. Usados inteligentemente, no cabe duda de que estos filtros modernos tienen un lugar en la fotografía creativa. Desafortunadamente, muchos de los ejemplos presentados este año para posible inclusión en el Anuario resultaron demasiado artificiosos como para justificar su aceptación.

Yo creo que los nuevos productos expuestos en la Feria de este año van a tener un impacto mayor en el Anuario 1985. Acabo de fotografiar la iluminación de Las Vegas con lente de foco regulable de 35–200mm, utilizando película de color ASA 1000 y una cámara totalmente programada, nada de lo cual se encontraba disponible hace un año. No cabe duda de que en muchos casos ahora se puede uno concentrar de verdad en la fotografía y dejar que la mecánica se encargue de lo demás. Esperemos que tales mejoras nos animen a aprovechar lo más posible nuestra imaginación creativa.

Me han preguntado en numerosas ocasiones si he disfrutado preparando esta edición del Anuario, y la respuesta es un rotundo sí. Para mí, la fotografía siempre ha sido sinónimo de magia y simplemente me encanta mirar fotos, y no cabe duda de que hubieron muchas que ver en las presentaciones de este año.

¿Qué me parece el nivel de aptitud? En general, lo encontré impresionante. Me causó una agradable sorpresa observar el elevado nivel de calidad del material en color presentado, a tal extremo que – en vista de tanto material en color de excelente calidad – se decidió a ñadir 16 páginas en colores al Anuario de este año.

El proceso de selección inicial de fotografías para el Anuario es muy parecido al que se adopta para grandes exposiciones, y – naturalmente – presentó los mismos probemas. En calidad de Redactor o de Adjudicador, ¿me incumbía elegir: a) las fotografías que más me gustaron, b) las que pensé que le gustarían más al público; o, c) las que yo creí que debiera ver el público? Al final casi omití las fotografías de las categorías b) y c). No creo que una publicación tal como el Anuario de la Fotografía debiera ser vehículo para sacar a relucir las injusticias sociales nacionales o internacionales ni los horrendos acontecimientos que vive continuamente el mundo. Ya se encargan de hacerlo diariamente nuestra TV y prensa. Quizás la única excepción sea la fotografía del huerfanito de Afganistán, por Mike Hollist del Daily Mail. La conmovedora expresión en la cara del niño le llegará al corazón a cualquier observador que vea la fotografía. Hace más de cuarenta años ví dos fotos que me causaron impresión para toda la vida, porque me hicieron ver que la fotografía es mucho más que simplemente sacar fotos. La primera fué una de una serie tomada en la región de las escritoras Bronte, por Bill Brandt, publicada en el Picture Post, y la segunda fué de huérfanitos refugiándose en una trinchera contra el atague de aviones alemanes mientras recogían lúpulo en un campo de Kent. Fué publicada en el Daily Mail a comienzos de la guerra, y la fotografía del huerfanito de Afganistán me causó la misma impresión profunda.

En el proceso de recopilación del libro, primero examiné todas las fotografías, presentadas en blanco y negro y en color y las clasifiqué en tres categorías: a) las que definitivamente creí que debieran ser incluidas en el Anuario; b) las que me gustaría incluir, de resultar posible; y c) las que se incluirían si conviniese para la preparación y formato del libro. A continuación subdividí estas fotografías en unas ocho sub-categorías: o sea, en paisajes, retratos, modelos etc. A la hora de preparar la disposición final del libro – debido al duplicado de temas, formato inadecuado, etc. – fué necesario descartar algunas de las fotos de la categoría a) y substituir algunas de la b) y de la c) para lograr un equilibrio global satisfactorio. Por desgracia, ésto significó que algunas fotos de excelente calidad tuvieron que ser omitidas pero – previa debida autorización del autor – algunas de éstas serán retenidas para posible inserción en la edición del año que viene.

No limité en absoluto el número de ejemplares presentados por cualquier fotógrafo determ-inado, ni tamboco me influenció el país de origen del material, al extremo de que no se hizo referencia alguna al dorso de la foto durante el proceso de selección y preparación del material.

¿Me hizo pensar el material presentado en algunas tendencias en la fotografía? En primer lugar, me sentí muy impresionado por la alta calidad del trabajo originario de los países de Europa Oriental, y de hecho el editor y yo visitamos Alemania, para asegurarnos de que recibiríamos una buena selección de los países del bloque comunista. Estas fotografías mostraron gran destreza e imaginación en la representación de temas cotidianos y ordinarios, y los fotógrafos de estos países parecen tomar fotos de todo – desde nacimientos a muertes – con el mismo entusiasmo. En segundo lugar, se observa una tendencia general a cuidar más la presentación de la fotografía, y muchas de las fotos presentadas llevaban un marco o ribete fotográficamente impreso. Por razones de preparación y disposición del material, en algunos casos hubo desafortunadamente que quitarse dicho marco o ribete.

Parece ser que el estilo de los últimos quince años más o menos, de producir las fotografías sin márgenes hasta el borde de la cartulina impresa, bien podría sufrir un cambio radical.

En tercer lugar, aún persiste una fuerte tendencia a producir fotografías de tono agudo o de intenso contraste con textura sobresaliente. Esta técnica indudablemente crea cierto impacto y resulta muy apta para ciertos temas. Sin embargo, en varios casos de fotos presentadas se utilizó esta técnica cuando el tema representado resultaba totalmente incompatible.

En conclusión, deseo expresar mi agradecimiento a todos los participantes que se molestaron en presentar material para posible inclusión en el Anuario de la Fotografía 1984. Mis felicitaciones a los que fueron aceptados y mis condolencias para los que no lo fueron. Finalmente, deseo rogar encarecidamente a todos a los que tuvieron éxito, a los que no lo tuvieron, y a todo aquél que crea que tiene material adecuado, que tenga la bondad de presentarlo para la edición de 1985.

Introduction du Rédacteur en Chef

Assis à écrire ces notes en contemplant Las Vegas de la fenêtre de ma chambre d'hôtel, venant de passer quatre jours à l'exposition de l'"Association de Commercialisation des Photos, je me demande quelle sera l'influence exercée sur la photographie pratique et la matière présentée pour les publications annuelles de l'avenir par les nouveaux produits vus à l'exposition.

En pensant à la même exposition de l'année dernière, on se souvient de l'impact irrésistible qu'a eu Kodak avec l'introduction de son appareil-photos à disque. Je ne me rappelle aucune des photos présentées cette année-ci qui ont été prises avec ce format. A mon avis il n'y a aucune raison pour laquelle ce format ne pourrait être exploité pour la réalisation sérieuse des images. Charles Weckler de New York a fait publier dans le magasine "Popular Photography" édition d'avril 1982, des photos pleines d'imagination et évocatrices d'humeur changeante, dont les négatifs ont été produits avec un appareil 110, et dont le grain produit en utilisant le film 400 ASA a contribué largement au sentiment évoqué par les images. Peut-être l'éditeur ou Kodak devrait-il accorder un prix au premier photographe à faire publier une photo "disque" dans l'Annuaire!

Il y a un an, une gamme d'appareils compacts 35mm est également parue et des photos prises avec ces appareils ont été présentées cette année, et un des photos prises avec ces appareils ont été presque impossible de prendre une certaine photo sans la vitesse de l'objectif autofocus. Il y a un an il a été présenté des appareils reflex à vitesse de 1/4000e maximum, ainsi que des appareils reflex cibernés de façon intelligente et autofocus ou mise à point assistée. Ces améliorations ont sans aucun doute un impact sur la photographie actuelle et quelques résultats ont été publiés dans l'édition de l'année courante.

Il a été mis en évidence tant à l'exposition de cette année qu'à l'exposition de l'année dernière des filtres de presque toutes les formes et tailles susceptibles de tout déformer depuis les couleurs jusqu'á la définition. Voilà, me semble-t-il les fabricants d'"objectifs et de film qui dépensent des sommes énormes pour améliorer la définition et le rendu des couleurs et d'autres fabricants qui sortent des produits pour faire pleinement le contraire! Utilisés de façon intelligente, ces filtres modernes ont certainement leur place dans la photographie créative. Malheureusement de nombreuses preuves soumises en vue de leur publication éventuelle dans l'édition de cette année étaient bien trop artificielles pour mériter d'être acceptées.

J'ai l'impression que les nouveaux produits mis en évidence à l'exposition de cette année auront un plus grand impact sur l'Annuaire de 1985. Je viens de photographier les lumières de Las Vegas avec un objectif à visée variable de 35-200mm, utilisant un film en couleurs 1000 ASA avec un appareil entièrement programmé, aucun de ces articles n'existant l'année précédente. Dans de nombreux cas, on peut maintenant de toute évidence se consacrer totalement à la photo pour permettre aux mécanismes d'assurer leurs fonctions. Espérons que de telles améliorations nous encourageront à utiliser pleinement notre imagination créatrice.

On m'a demandé de nombreuses fois si j'avais pris plaisir à assembler cette édition de l'Annuaire, et la réponse est un oui énergique. Pour moi, la photographie a toujours été magique et cela me donne une joie profonde de regarder des photos, et il y en avait certainement beaucoup à regarder parmi les soumissions de cette année.

Et la qualité? Elle était en grande partie assez impressionnante. J'ai été agréablement surpris par la haute qualité des oeuvres présentées et il a été en fait décidé, en vue de tant d'excellente matière en couleurs, d'augmenter de 16 le nombre des pages en couleur dans l'annuaire courant.

La sélection initiale des photos pour l'"Annuaire se fait de façon bien semblable à celle des photos pour une grande exposition et cela a bien entendu posé les mêmes problèmes. Est-ce que je devais, en qualité d'Editeur ou d'Arbitre, choisir a) les photos qui me plaisaient, b) celles qui selon mon avis plairaient aux spectateurs, ou bien c) les photos que selon moi, les spectateurs devraient voir. En fin de compte j'ai presque omis d'inclure des photos rentrant en catégories b) et c). Je ne crois pas qu'une publication telle que l'Annuaire Photographique doive être un véhicule pour exposer les injustices sociales nationales ou internationales ni les événements honorifiques du monde, puisque ces phénomènes sont couverts tous les jours par nos journaux et la télévision. Une exception peut-être, ce serait la photo d'un orphelin afghan prise par Mike Hollist du Daily Mail – la mine touchante du garçon doit déchirer le coeur de tout spectateur. Il y a plus de quarante ans, j'ai vu deux photos qui ont influencé ma vie entière parce qu'elles m'ont révélé que la photographie est beaucoup plus que de simples instantanés. La première faisait partie d'un suite de photos sur la région des Brontë, réalisé par Bill Brandt, publiée dans le Picture Post, et l'autre représentant de petits orphelins s"abritant dans une tranchée contre des avions allemands lors d'une cueillette du houblon dans le Kent. Cette photo avait été publiée dans le Daily Mail au cours des premiers jours de la guerre et la photo de l'orphelin afghan a provoqué la même impression.

En composant le livre, j'ai parcouru d'abord toutes les photos, monochromes et en couleurs, je les ai présentées et réparties en trois catégories a) pour les photos qui pensais-je catégoriquement, devraient être incluses, b) pour les photos que je voudrais inclure si possible, et c) celles qui seraient inclues si cela facilitait l'aménagement. J'ai donc sous-divisé ces images en huit catégories environ, á savoir, paysages, portraits, motif etc. Lorsqu'il en est venu à l'aménagement définitif, il est devenu nécessaire, du fait de répétition de sujets, format peu approprié, de laisser tomber quetques-unes des photos de la catégorie a) et de les remplacer par quelques-unes de catégories b) et c) pour obtenir une bonne harmonie. Malheureusement cela a entrainé la suppression d'un petit nombre de photos excellentes, et avec la permission de l'auteur quelques-unes de ces dernières seront réservées pour leur publication éventuelle dans l'édition de l'année prochaine.

En matière de l'importance de la représentation dans le livre d'un photographe individuel, je n'y ai imposé aucune limite, et aucune influence n'a été non plus exercée sur moi en ce qui concerne le pays d'origine. En fait aucune référence n'a été faite au dos de la photo lors de la selection et de l'aménagement.

Les soumissions m'ont-elles donné une indication de tendances photographiques? D'abord, la haute qualité des oeuvres en provenance de l'Europe Orientale m'a bien impressionné. En fait, l'éditeur et moi avons visité l'Allemagne pour nous assurer la réception d'un bon choix de photos des pays du Bloc de l'Europe Orientale. Ces photos accusaient une adresse et une imagination en matière de sujets assez ordinaires et les photographes de ces pays semblaient photographier le tout depuis la naissance jusqu'à la mort avec le même enthousiasme. Deuxièment, il y a une plus grande tendance de la part des photographes en général, à se donner plus de peine pour la présentation de leurs photos, et beaucoup des preuves réussies qui ont été présentées avaient le bord imprimé de façon photographique. Malheureusement aux fins de l'aménagement, il a fallu éliminer ce bord.

Il me semble que le style de photos à pleins bords de la dernière quinzaine d'années pourra bien subir un changement radical.

Troisièment il existe toujours une tendance marquée à produire des images heurtées ou dures avec un grain manifeste. Cette technique crée certainement un impact et elle est appropriée à certains sujects. Pourtant un nombre de photos présentées, cette technique a été utilisée alors qu'elle était bien incompatible avec le sujet.

En conclusion, je voudrais remercier tous ceux qui se sont donné la peine de présenter la matière pour une publication éventuelle dans l'Annuaire Photographique 1984. Mes félicitations à ceux dont les photos ont été acceptées, mes condoléances à ceux qui n'ont pas réussi, et une demande très sincères aux reçus et non-reçus et à tous ceux qui pensent disposer de sujets appropriés de bien vouloir faire des soumissions pour l'édition de 1985.

Task-Self Portrait Hang Gliding

Canon NEW F-1

EQUIPMENT
New F-1 with AE Finder centre-weighted metering type focusing screen and Power Winder FN bolted to wing strut of glider. Lens FD 15mm f 2.8 full-frame fish eye.

TECHNIQUE
Camera fired by pilot using remote control lead. Shutter speed pre-selected at 1/500 seconds and aperture controlled automatically by the camera.

By using the new F-1 with its modular exposure system, you can have the precise photographic instrument that you require. No other professional system can offer this degree of versatility.

The new F-1 is, in its simplest form, a superbly precise manual camera.

With the AE Finder fitted later or as standard, the camera also offers aperture priority automation as well as complete manual control. Add the Motor Drive FN or Power Winder FN and shutter priority automation is available, plus aperture priority, plus manual.

The New F-1 system also includes: 5 interchangeable finders, 32 focusing screens, bulk and data back, various remote control devices and over 50 FD lenses.

Canon (UK) Ltd., Camera Division,
Brent Trading Centre, North Circular Road, Neasden NW10 0JF

Canon
The ultimate camera choice.

Canon - manufacturers of Cameras, Calculators, Copiers, Computers, Typewriters, Facsimile business machines and Microfilm

Jánis Gleizds

as Kalvelis   Chris Thurman

Bill Cross

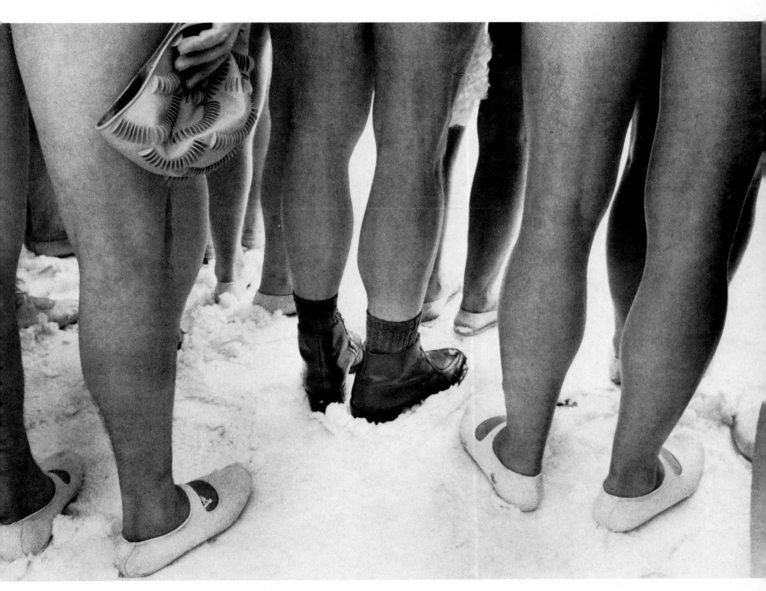

Oleg Homola

David Rice-Evans

Clive B Harrison

Mervyn Rees

Werner Stuhler

28/29   Adrian Murrell

30/31 Valdis Brauns/A Markey

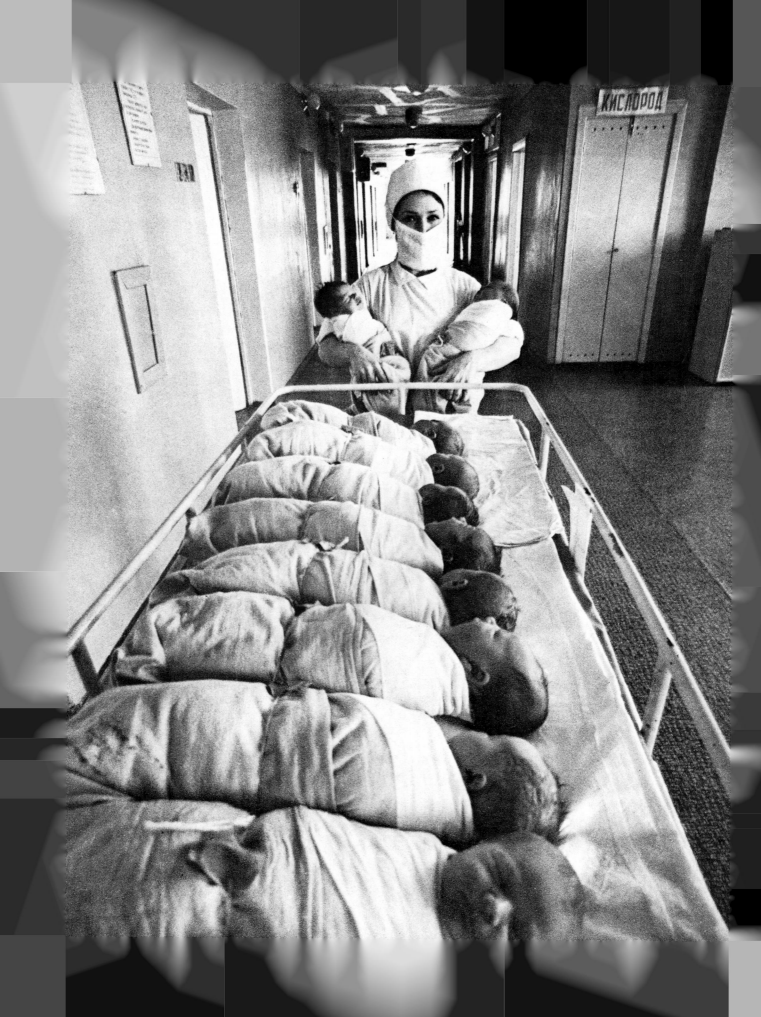

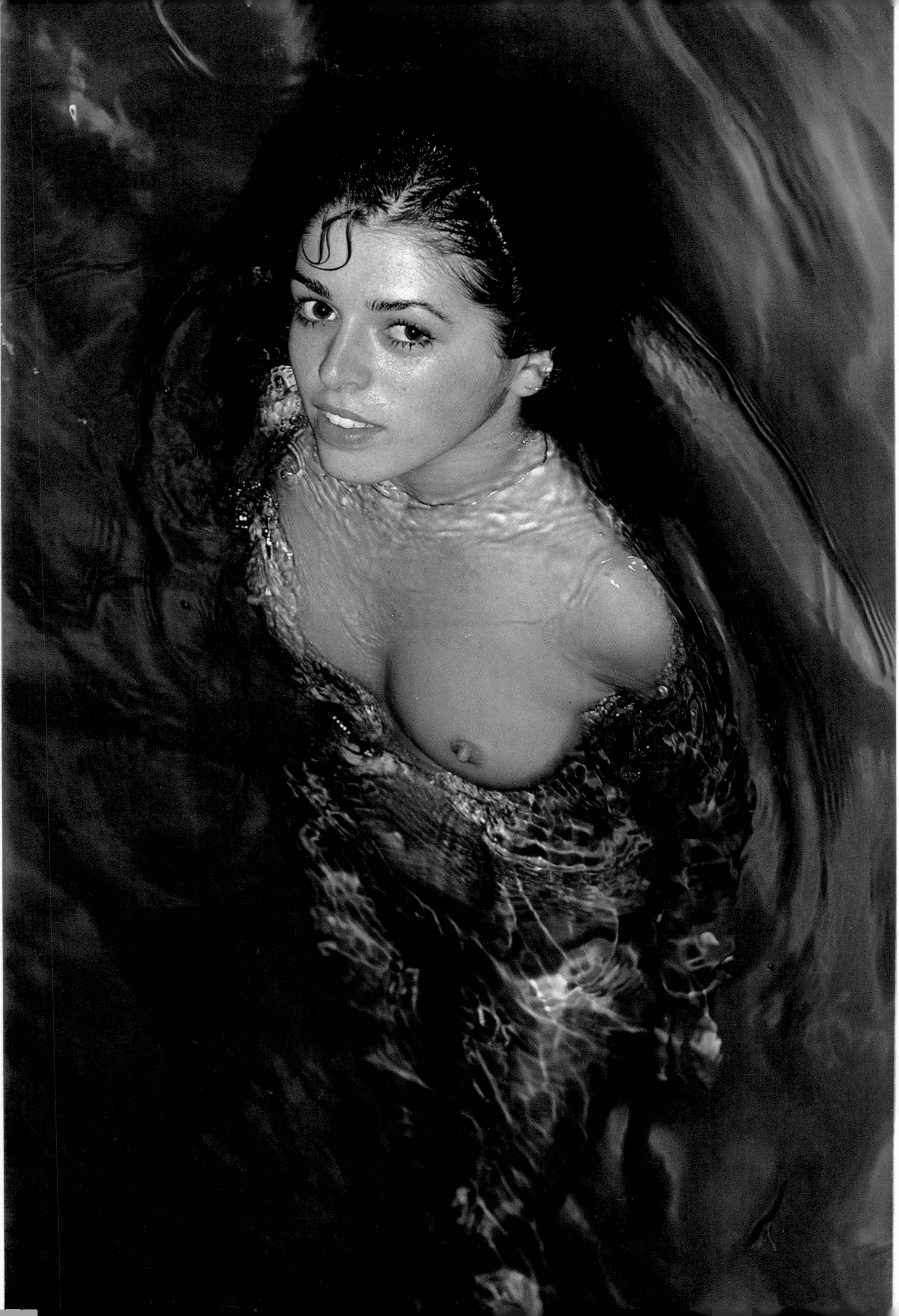

C J Stratmann

34

Dr Leo KK Wong

Colin Westgate

Antonio Bonet Rius

M Van Den Heuvel

Ken Deitcher

43

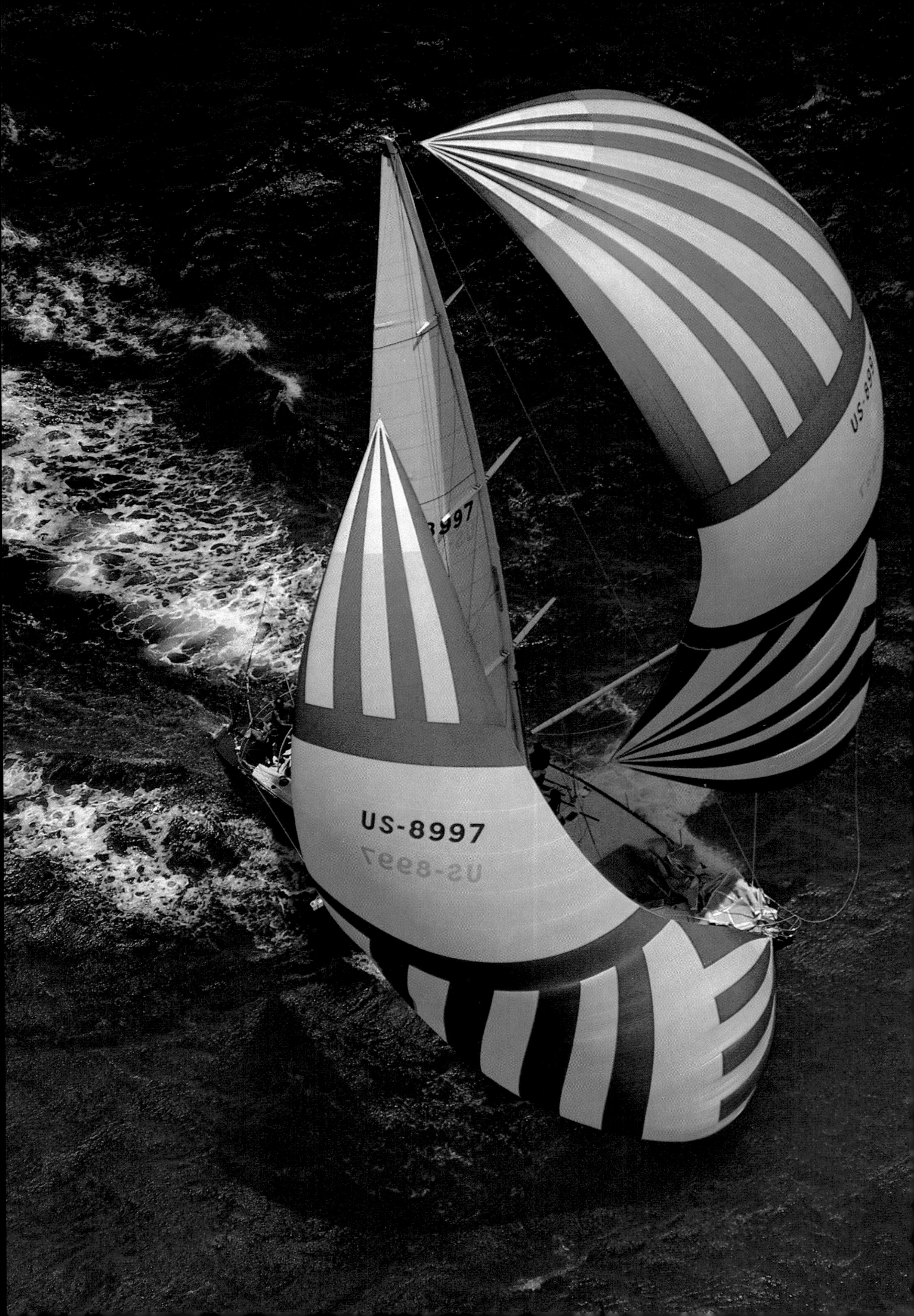
US-8997
8997

Stanley Matchett

46

HSFry

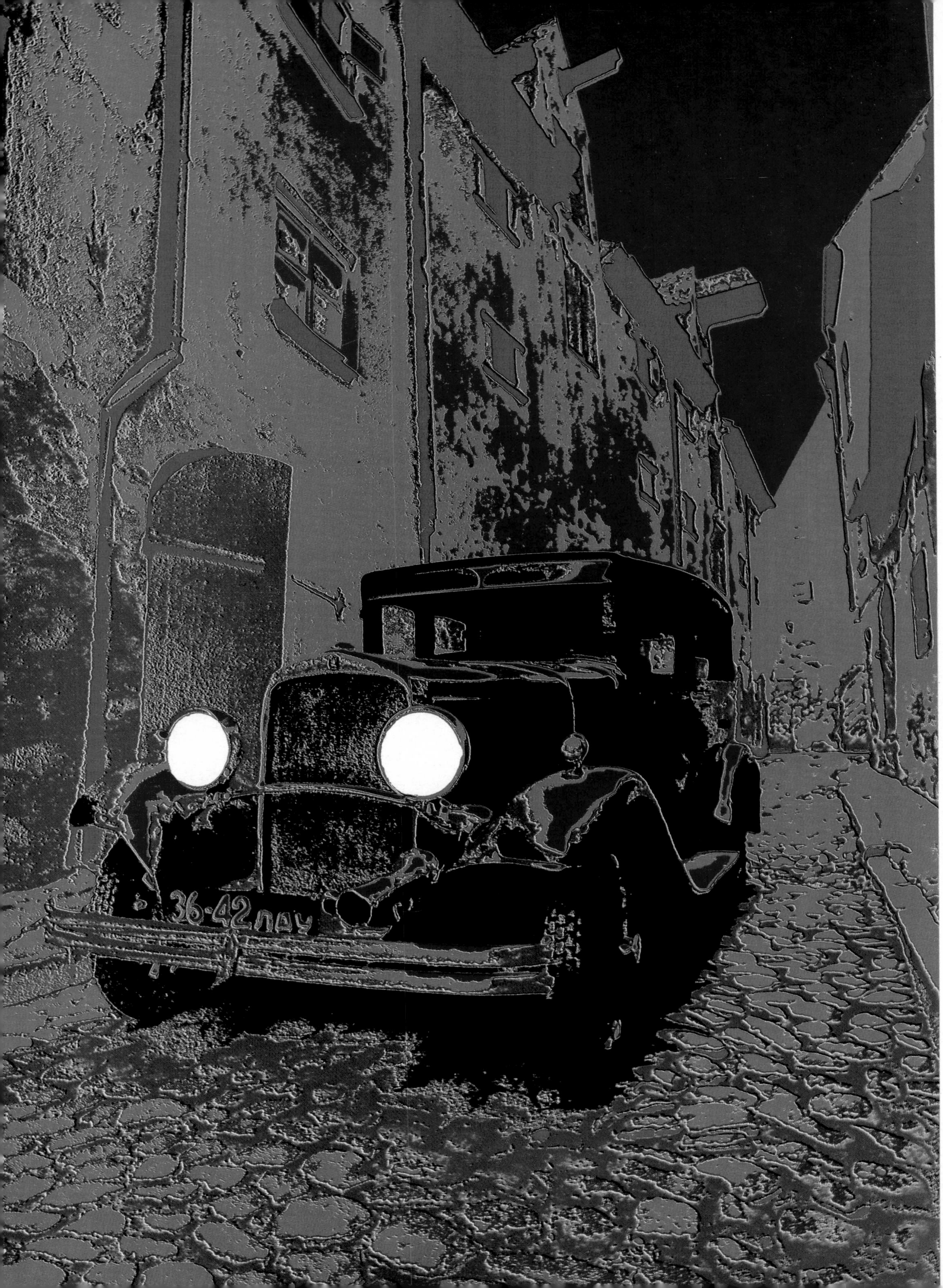

Jánis Gailitis 48

Enzo Lombardi

Dennis Mansell

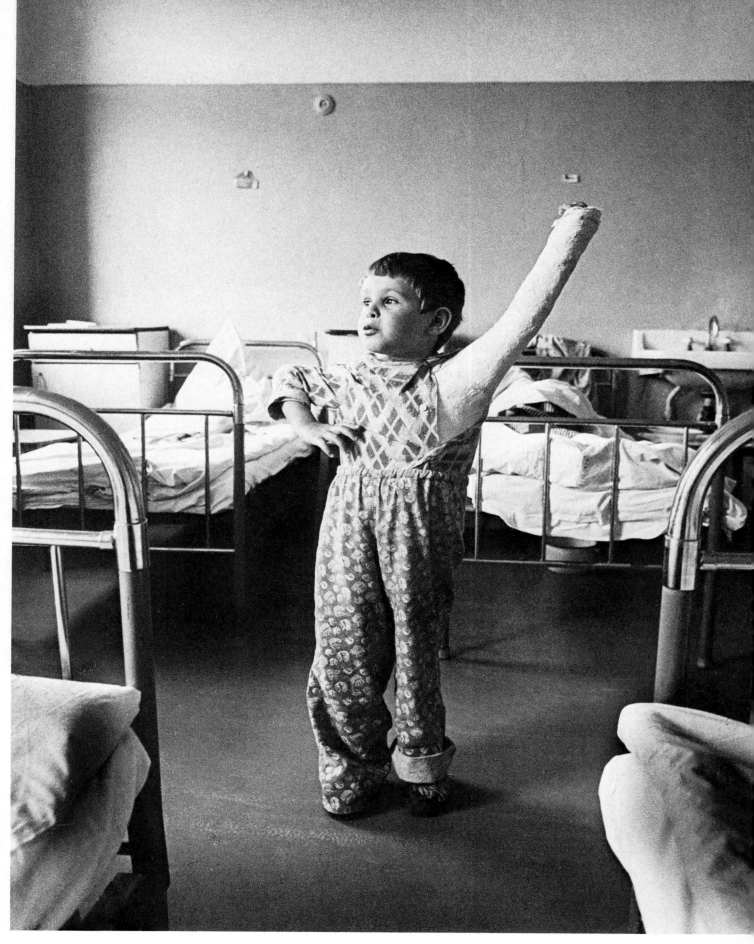

Romualdos Požerskis

Helene Rogers

52

53 Walter Schollmayer

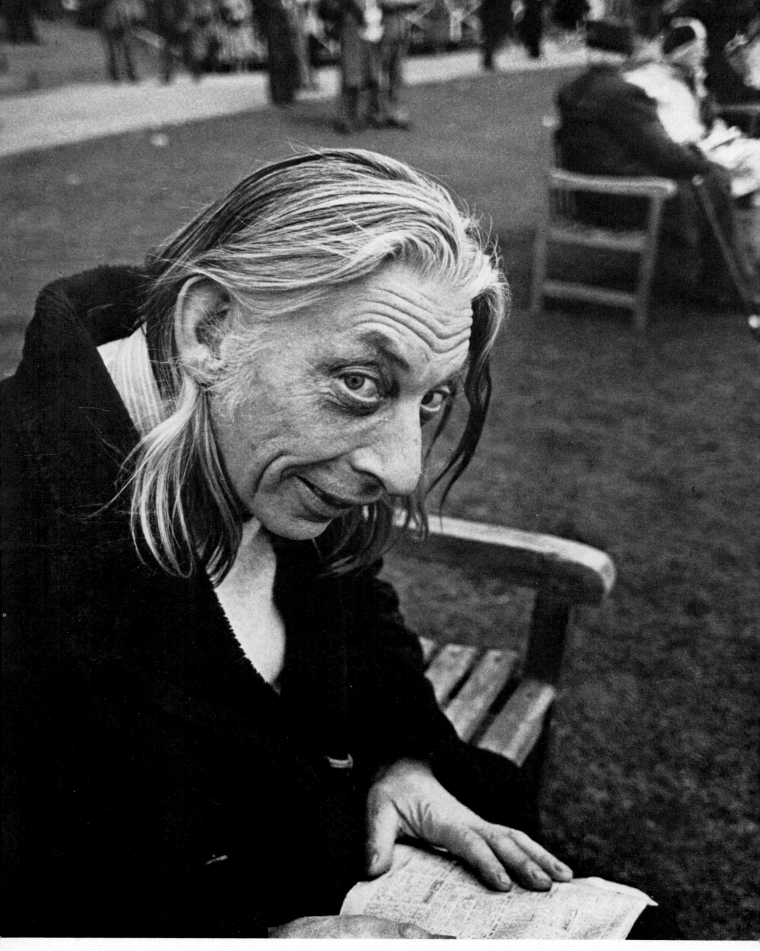

Joan Wakelin

Bob Moore

Denis Thorpe

Antonio Grau i Lopez

John Russell

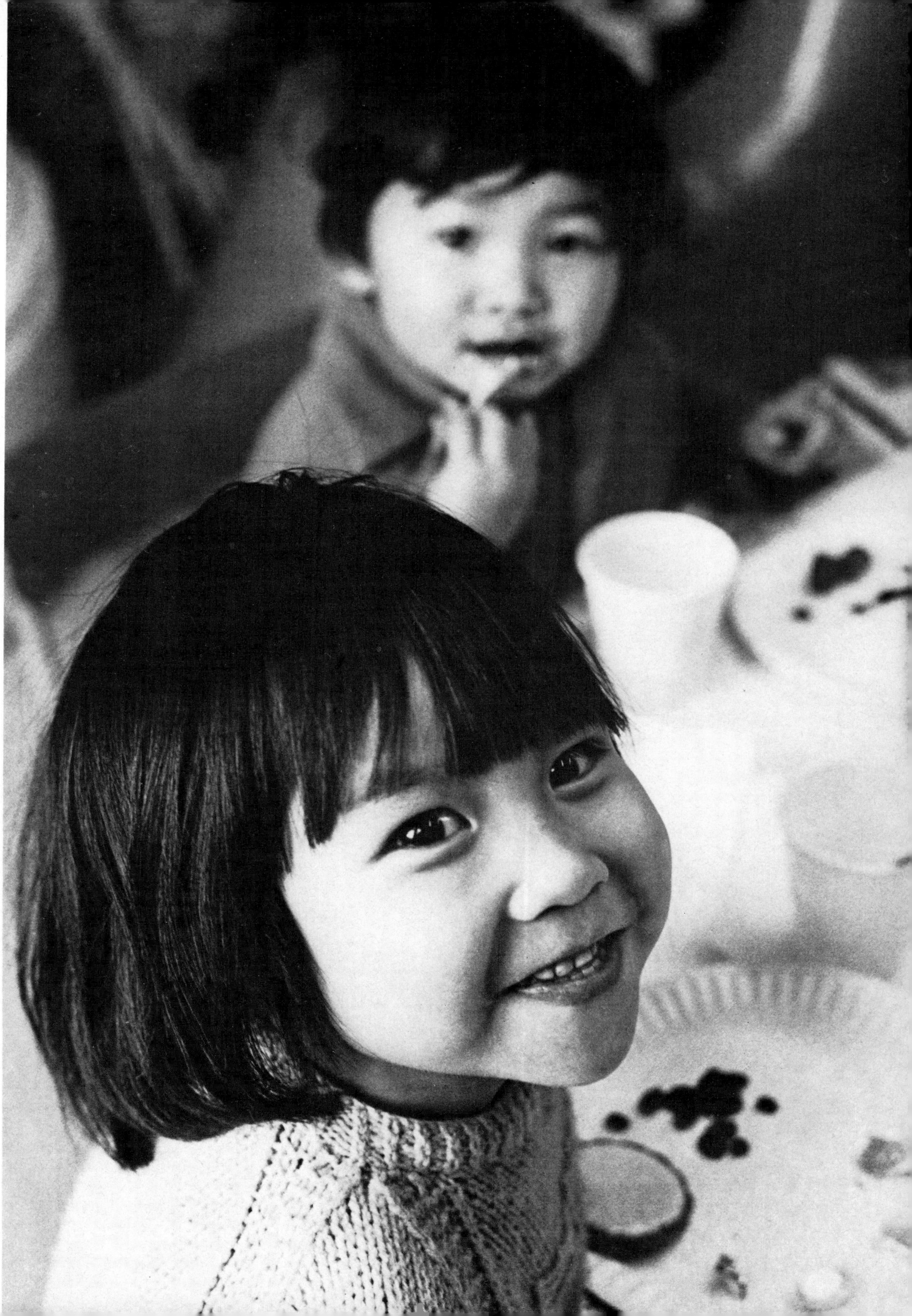

59 Asadour Guzelian

A Bareišis   Doug Chalk

Brian Scott   Denny Rowland

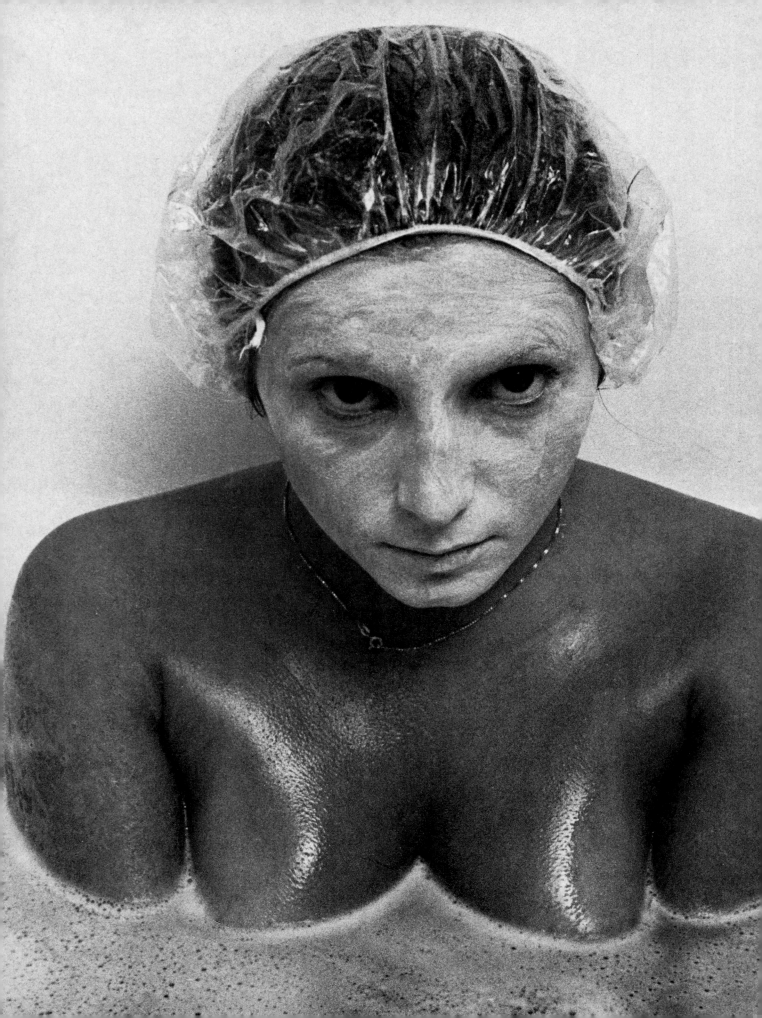

John Davidson John Davidson

Bernard Lequint

David Chamberlain

Chas Thompson

Manuel Monjibar Cortes

Derek J Grant

Andrej Krynicki

Stanislaw Trzaska

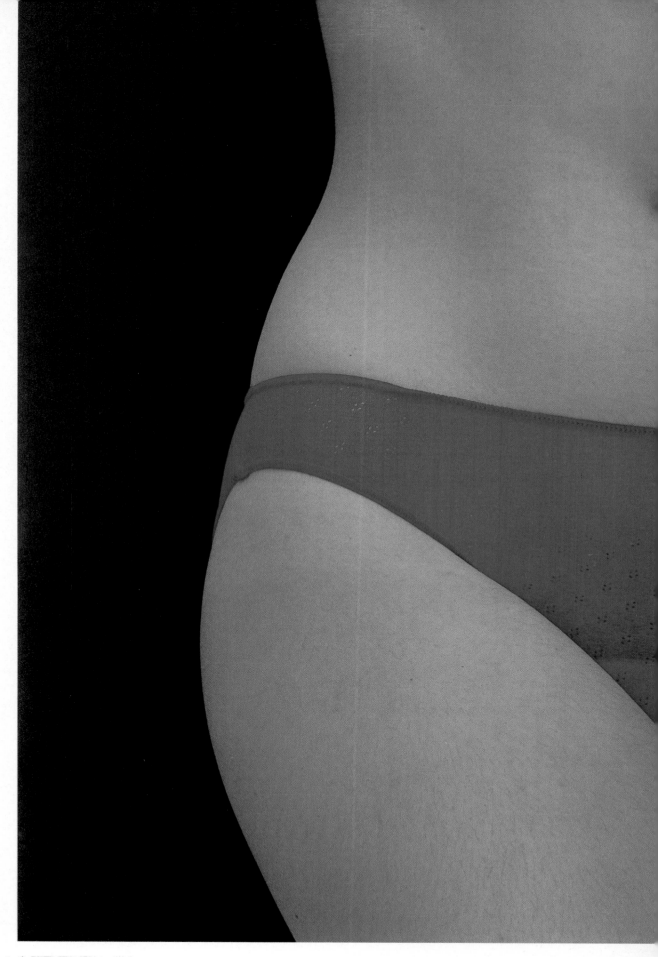

Antonio Rius

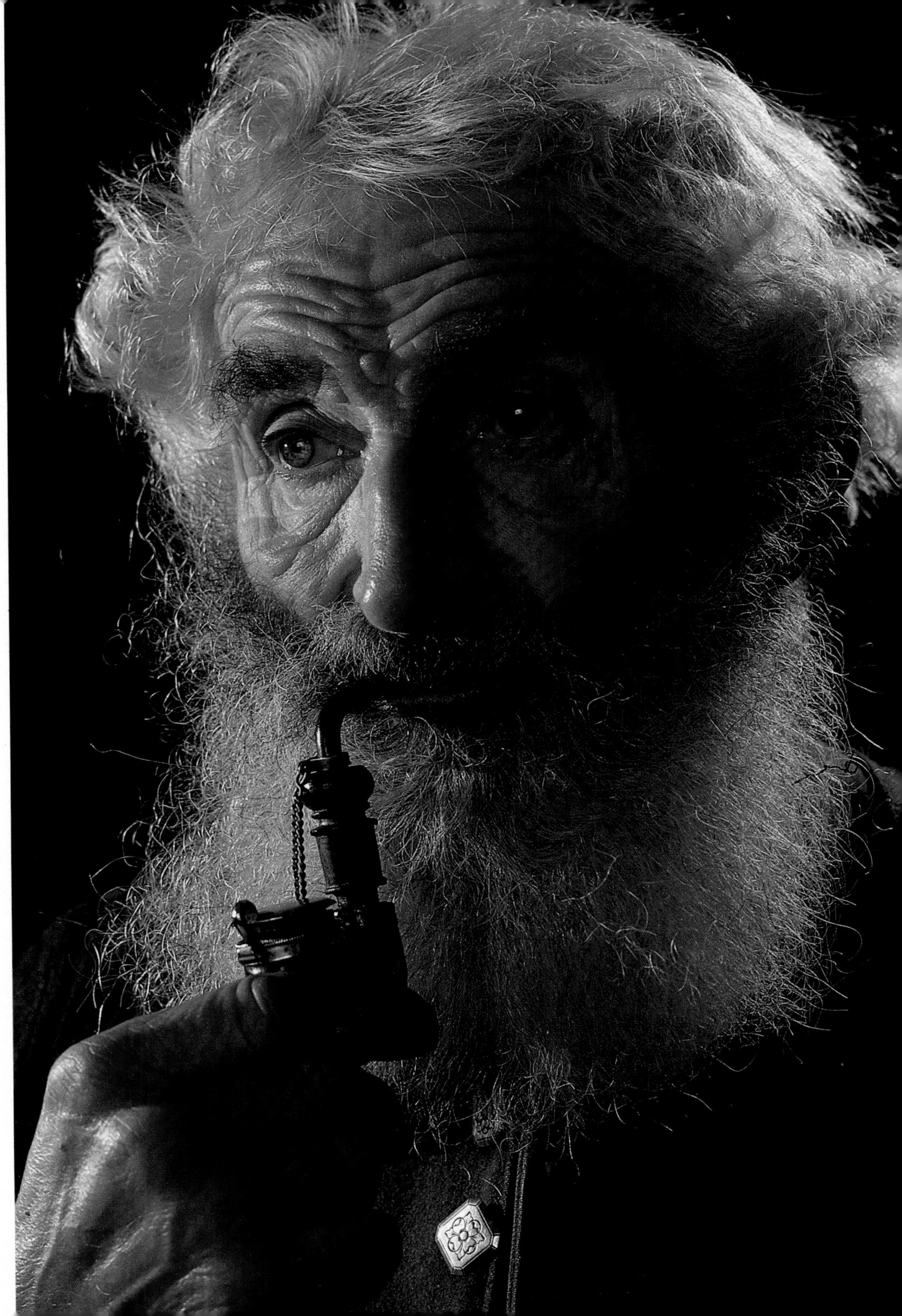

Max Hess

Michel Celérier

Serge Guiolet

Erik Steen

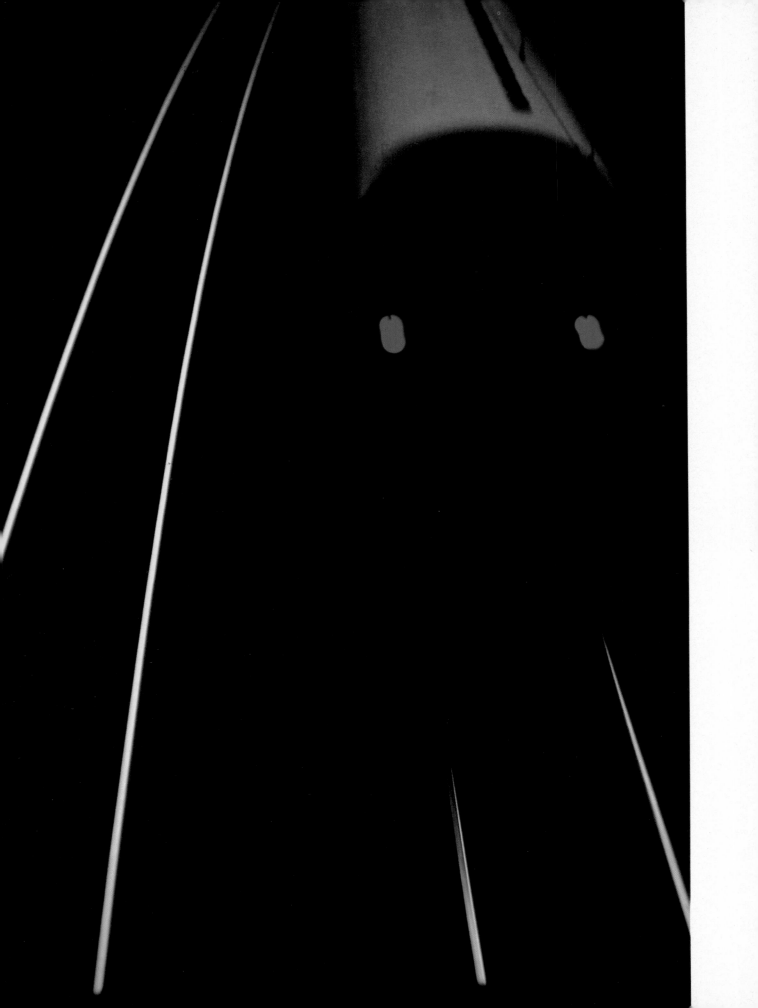

Steve Powell

David Higgs

96

Mayotte Magnus

Naresh Sohal

Mike Taylor

Vlado Bača

Vlado Bača

Ian Spratt

104

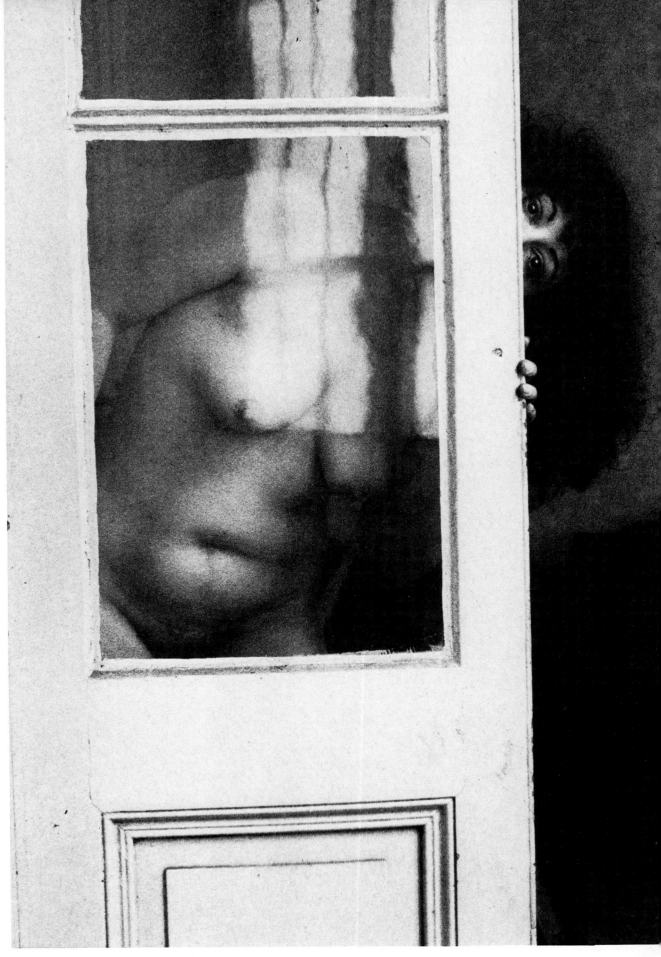

Max Fund

Howard Walker

Stephen Shakeshaft

Jenifer Roberts

S. Paul

Manfred Fitzner

Peeter Langovits

Tony Ward

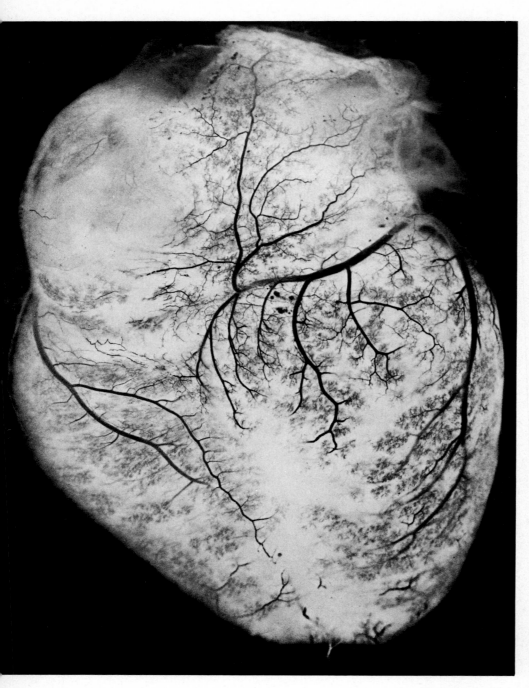

Kevin Fitzpatrick   Hans-Ulrich Comberg

Bodo Goeke

James Meehan

Mike Hollist

Eddie Brown

Branko Težak 121

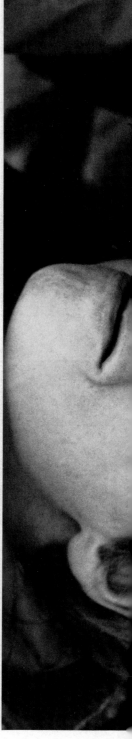

Clive B Harrison   S. Riley

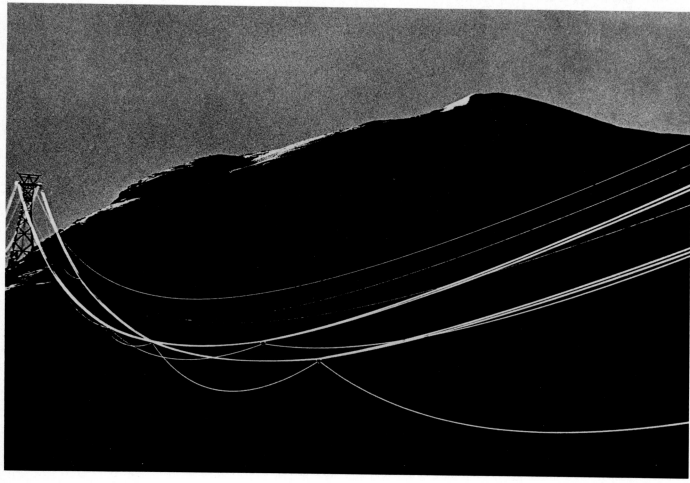

126/127 Giuseppe Balla

Bruce Lloyd

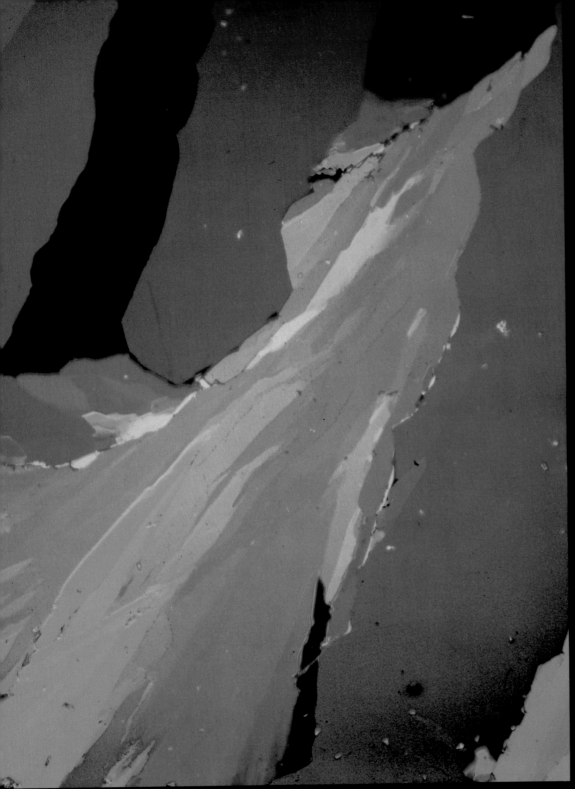

C J Kocher

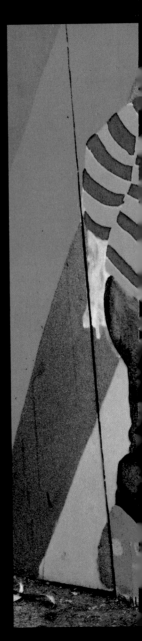

Daniel Chenu

Jorge Lewinski

Mike Brett

Peter M Rees

Christain Him

140

P S Clay

Mike Brett 142

Robert Hallman

J W Legate

Bob Gray

145

Mike Brett

Mike Brett

Mike Hollist   A. Markey

153

156   Josep Maria Ribas i Prous

Oldřich Karásek

157

W.O. Turnbull

Denis Thorpe

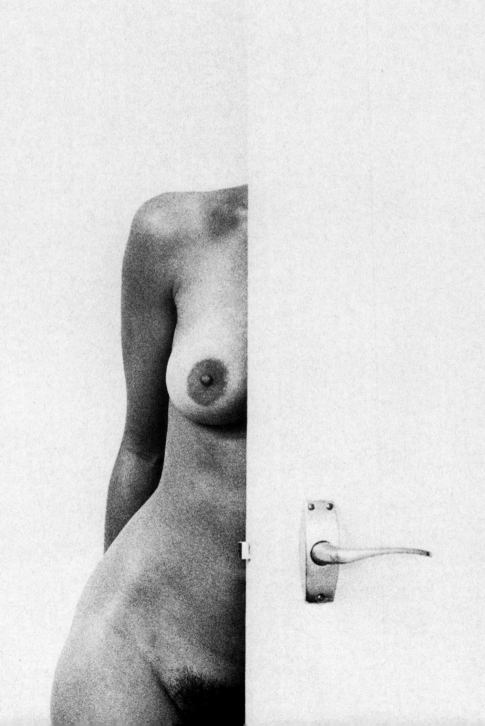

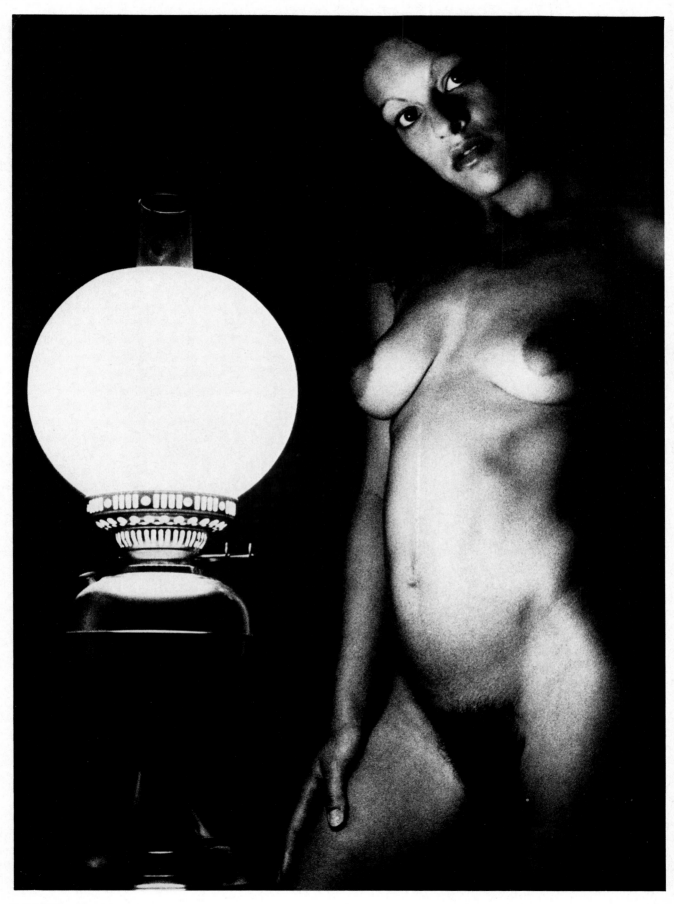

David Chamberlain

Gary Browne

Oleg Homola

Oleg Homola

T.S. Norton

Neale Davison

Neale Davison

Tracey Chamberlain   Keith Brown

174

Christian Vogt

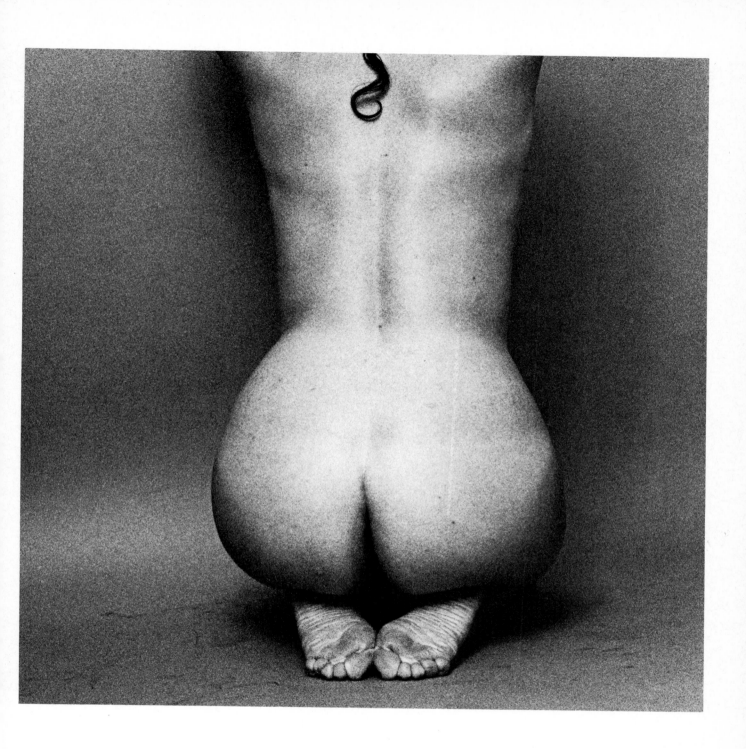

Benito Moya Vivar

Tony Ward

Dieter Neumann

Derek Grant

W H Murenbleed

Pedro Raota

N G Patel

Peter Tryuk

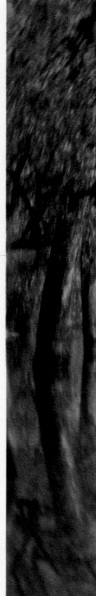

Sandor Rozaś

R M Johnson

Veikko Wallström

Jacki Sime

D Whiteoak

Stephen Shakeshaft

194/Antanas Sutkus

195/Leona Korkutiene

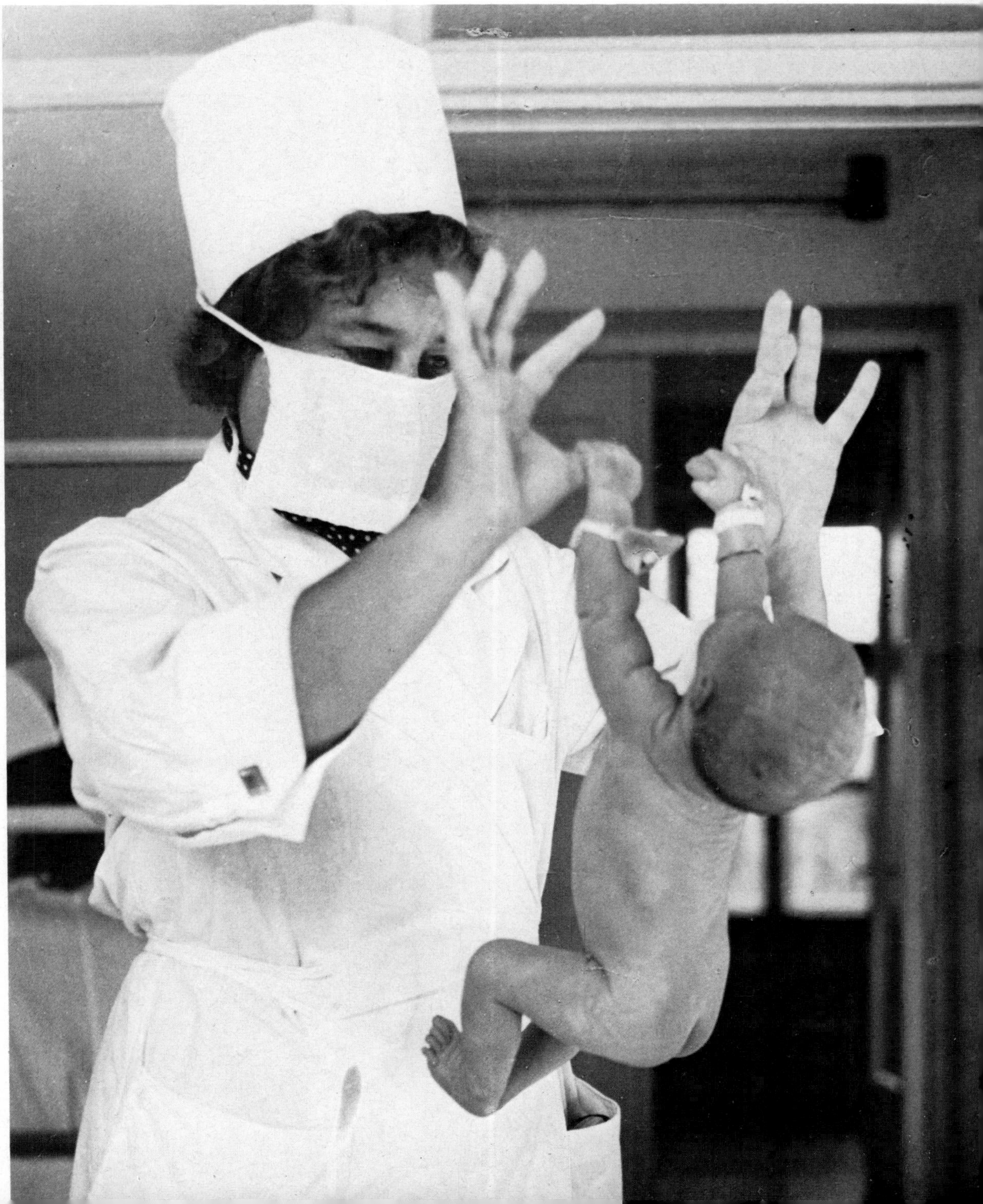

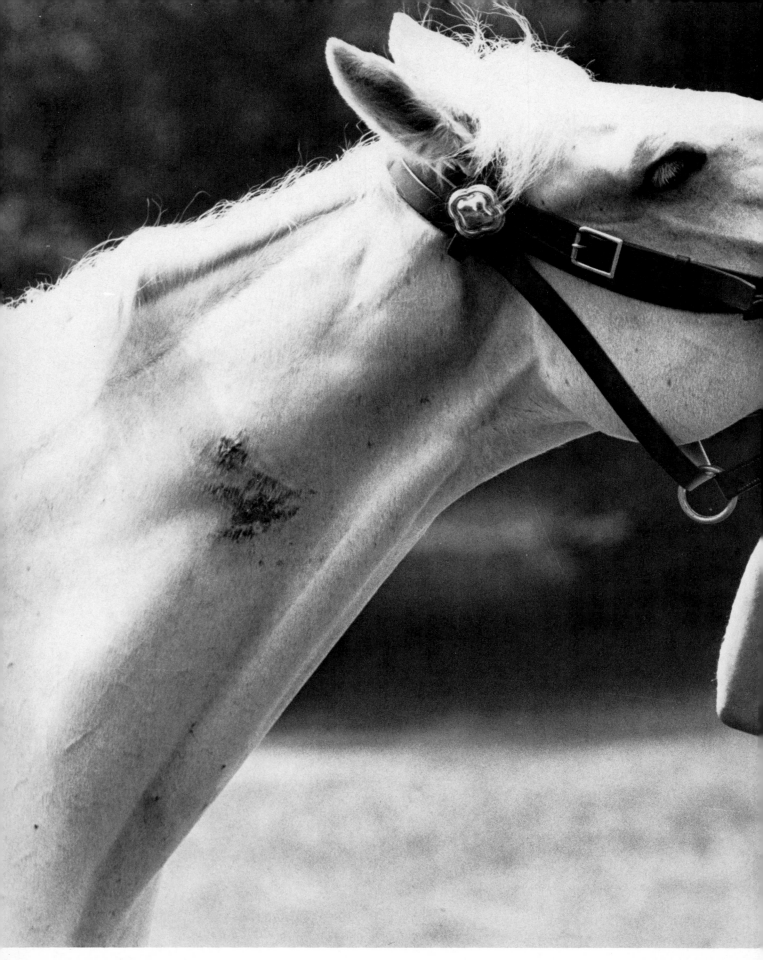

196/197   Mike Hollist

Jane Millar

Veikko Wallström

Veikko Wallström

202 Arnold Umlauf

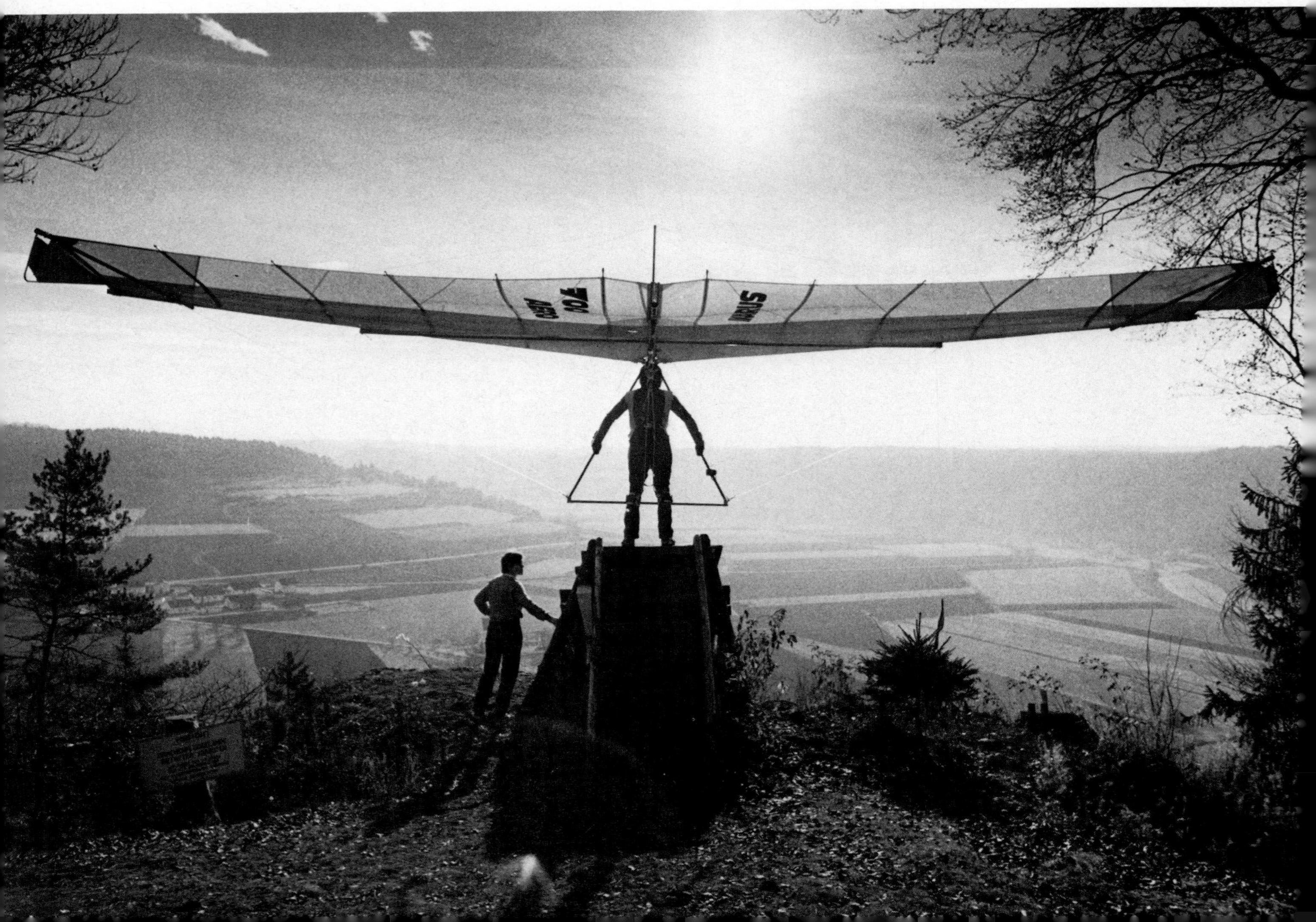

Asadour Guzelian

UNDER
2 HRS

František Dostál

Martin J O'Neill

Hansjochen Heinecke

Hansjochen Heinecke

Manfred Gsteu

Colin Westgate

Hans-Ulrich Comberg

Richard Summersby

Neale Davison

Howard Walker

218

Karl Ziegler

Ole Sand

Jagdish Agarwal

224

Romnaldas Poźerskis

226

Antonio Grau i Lopez

Technical Data

Jacket

Title	Condor
Photographer	Alastair Black (UK)
Camera	Nikon
Lens	105 mm.
Film	Kodachrome 64

Front End Paper

Title	'High And Dry'
Photographer	K. R. Brown FRPS (UK)
Camera	Minolta KG 2
Lens	28 mm Rokkor
Film	FP 4

15

Title	'The Flower'
Photographer	Jānis Gleizds (Estonia – USSR)
Camera	
Lens	Tech. data not supplied
Film	

16

Title	'Dunes'
Photographer	Jonas Kalvelis (Lithuania – USSR)
Camera	Pentacon Six
Lens	50 mm Flektogon
Film	Foto 65

17

Title	'Seascape—Ostende'
Photographer	Chris Thurman ARPS (UK)
Camera	Rolleiflex T
Lens	Tech. data not supplied
Film	Tri–X

18/19

Title	'A Drop of Beaujolais'
Photographer	Bill Cross (UK)
Camera	
Lens	Tech. data not supplied
Film	

20

Title	'Riding High'
Photographer	Günther Prätor (D.D.R)
Camera	Orwo NP 20/KB
Lens	Sonar 3.5/135 mm
Film	Tech. data not supplied

21

Title	'Much To Cold'
Photographer	Oleg Homola (Czechoslovakia)
Camera	
Lens	Tech. data not supplied
Film	

22

Title	'Skinheads on Bank Holiday in Southend'
Photographer	David Rice-Evans (UK)
Camera	Nikon F 2A
Lens	105 mm
Film	HP 5

23

Title	'Police Can-Can in Oxford Street'
Photographer	Clive B Harrison FRPS (UK)
Camera	Olympus OM1
Lens	28 mm – 2,8 Zuiko
Film	XP1 – 400

24

Title	'A Novice Diver At Crystal Palace'
Photographer	Mervyn Rees (UK)
Camera	Nikon F2
Lens	135 mm Nikkor
Film	Tri–X

25

Title	'Seagulls'
Photographer	Werner Stuhler (West Germany)
Camera	Hasselblad 500 C
Lens	BL ll
Film	HP 5

26

Title	'Singer and Actress Barbara Dickson in the Coffee Bar of The Playhouse Threatre, Liverpool'
Photographer	Brian Duff FRPS (UK)
Camera	Nikon F2
Lens	105 mm
Film	Tri–X

27

Title	Actor John Alderton caught during a break in filming
Photographer	Brian Duff FRPS (UK)
Camera	Nikon F
Lens	105 mm
Film	Tri–X

28/29

Title	'Pakistan Dispair'
Photographer	Adrian Murrell (UK)
Camera	
Lens	Tech. data not supplied
Film	

30

Title	'Rain Of Happiness'
Photographer	Valdis Brauns AFIAP (Latvia, USSR)
Camera	
Lens	Tech. data not supplied
Film	

31

Title	'Summer Holiday'
Photographer	A Markey
Camera	Nikon F2
Lens	Tech. data not supplied
Film	HP 5

32

Photographer	(From Russia)
Camera	
Lens	Tech. data not supplied
Film	

33
Title	'The Gown Of Water'
Photographer	C.J. Stratmann (UK)
Camera	
Lens	Tech. data not supplied
Film	

34
Title	'Fishing At Morn'
Photographer	Dr Leo K.K. Wong (Hong Kong)
Camera	Hasselblad
Lens	120 mm
Film	Kodacolor II

35
Title	'Storm Force 10 Newhaven'
Photographer	Colin Westgate (UK)
Camera	Konica T.C.
Lens	Vivitar 100 mm
Film	Agfachrome 50S Cibachrome

36 Upper
Title	'Sunshade & Palm'
Photographer	J. W. Legate (UK)
Camera	Pentax Spotmatic 1000
Lens	55 mm
Film	Kodachrome 64

36 Lower
Photographer	Geoffrey Giles (UK)
Camera	Nikon F3
Lens	Nikon Nikkor 55 mm. f/3.5 Micro lens
Film	3M Color Reversal 100

37
Photographer	Kent Bailey (USA)
Camera	Tech. data not supplied
Lens	Tech. data not supplied
Film	Kodachrome 64

38
Title	'Mama Nina'
Photographer	Antonio Bonet Rius (Spain)
Camera	Nikon F.E
Lens	135 mm Nikkor
Film	Kodachrome 64

39
Title	'Jonneke'
Photographer	M. Van Den Heuvel (Netherland)
Camera	Praktica LLC
Lens	Tech. data not supplied
Film	Agfa CT 18

40/41
Title	'Dal Lake Kashmir – The Flower Market'
Photographer	John Austin Locke (UK)
Camera	Nikon FE
Lens	80-200mm
Film	Ektachrome 64

42
Title	'Kingfisher on route to nest with fish for young'
Photographer	E.A. Janes (UK)
Camera	Haselblad
Lens	250 mm
Film	Agfa CT 18

43
Title	'Red Eyed Tree Frog'
Photographer	Ken Deitcher (USA)
Camera	Canon A1
Lens	Vivitar 70-210 macro-zoom
Film	Fujichrome 100

44 Upper
Title	'Windsurfer'
Photographer	Alastair Black
Camera	Sandwich transparency using Nikonos and Nikon F3
Lens	35 mm
Film	Kodachrome 64

44 Lower
Title	'Crowded Scene In Hawaian Surf'
Photographer	Alastair Black
Camera	Nikon F3
Lens	600 mm, with converter
Film	Kodachrome 64

45
Title	'Bull Frog Clipper Cup Hawai'
Photographer	Alastair Black (UK)
Camera	Nikon F3
Lens	105 mm
Film	Kodachrome 64

46
Title	'Sunday Morning in Old Madrid'
Photographer	Stanley Machett (UK)
Camera	Nikon FM2
Lens	80 – 200 m zoom
Film	Ektachrome 64

47
Title	'Hill Street'
Photographer	H.S. Fry (UK)
Camera	
Lens	Tech. data not supplied
Film	

48
Photographer	Jānis Gailitis (USSR)
Camera	
Lens	Tech. data not supplied
Film	

49
Title	'Rain Drops on the Window'
Photographer	Enzo Lombardi (Italy)
Camera	Pentax LX
Lens	50 mm Macro
Film	Ilford Pan F

Rollei

Growing in Range and Reputation

The Rolleiflex SL66E

New for '83

Launched at Photokina '82 the Rolleiflex SL66E medium format SLR camera incorporates electronic TTL light metering and dedicated flash metering.

The Rolleiflex SL2000F

With interchangeable magazines, two integral viewfinders, built-in motordrive, plus many more features, the launch of the SL2000F represents a major breakthrough in 35mm photography.

The Rolleiflex SL66

Incorporates built-in bellows with tilt facility, the SL66 is still one of the world's most unique medium format cameras (except for the SL66E).

The Rolleiflex SLX

With full electronic control of all camera functions the SLX is without doubt the most advanced 6 x 6cm camera available.

The Rollei range proves that in 1983 there is no better name to be seen with.

FOR FURTHER DETAILS PLEASE CONTACT A V DISTRIBUTORS (LONDON) LTD, 21 & 22 ST ALBANS PLACE, ISLINGTON, N1 0NX

50

Photographer	Dennis Mansell AIIP ARPS (UK)
Camera	Pentax
Lens	28 mm
Film	Tri–X

51

Title	'In The Hospital'
Photographer	Romnaldas Požerskis (Lithuania – U.S.S.R.)
Camera	Minolta XD II
Lens	28 mm Rokkor
Film	Orwo KN 3

52

Title	'Omdurman Cattle Market' Sudan
Photographer	Helene Rogers ARPS (UK)
Camera	Olympus OMI
Lens	135 mm
Film	FP 4

53

Title	'Sunrise in the Atlas Mountains'
Photographer	Walter Schollmayer (West Germany)
Camera	Nikon FM 2
Lens	135 mm Nikkor
Film	Tri–X

54

Title	'Studying the Form'
Photographer	Joan Wakelin FRPS (UK)
Camera	Canon AE I
Lens	24 mm
Film	Tri–X

55

Photographer	Bob Moore FRPS (UK)
Camera	Nikon FE
Lens	135 mm
Film	FP 4

56 Upper

Title	'Countryside Near Compiegne In France'
Photographer	Denis Thorpe (UK)
Camera	Nikon F2
Lens	35 mm
Film	FP 4

56 Lower

Photographer	Antonio Grau i Lopez (Spain)
Camera	
Lens	Tech. data not supplied
Film	

57

Title	'Great Missenden – Buckinghamshire'
Photographer	John Russel (UK)
Camera	Pentax 6 x 7
Lens	Tech. data not supplied
Film	FP 4

58

Title	'Lengwe National Park – Malawi'
Photographer	Jenifer Roberts ARPS (UK)
Camera	Olympus OM2
Lens	Tamron Adaptal 75–210 zoom
Film	Tri–X

59

Title	'Vietnamese Children in Bradford'
Photographer	Asadour Guzelian (UK)
Camera	Pentax K1000
Lens	50 mm
Film	Tri–X

60/61

Title	'A Battle Of Wits'
Photographer	Manfred Gsteu AFIAP (Austria)
Camera	Minolta XE–1
Lens	135 mm Rokkor Tele
Film	FP 4

62

Title	'A Difference In Taste'
Photographer	Algimantas Bareišis (Lithuania – USSR)
Camera	
Lens	Tech. data not supplied
Film	

63

Title	'Who's A Pretty Boy, Then?'
Photographer	Doug Chalk (UK)
Camera	Canon Sureshot
Lens	38 mm
Film	FP 4

64

Title	'To The Rescue'
Photographer	Brian Scott (Australia)
Camera	Nikon FM
Lens	200 mm
Film	HP 5

65

Title	'The Wrapp'
Photographer	Denny Rowland (UK)
Camera	Pentax 6 x 7
Lens	300 mm
Film	Tri–X

66

Title	'Well Groomed Lady'
Photographer	Stanislaw Trzaska (Poland)
Camera	Nikon FE
Lens	35 mm
Film	Tri–X

67

Photographer	Andrzej Sawa (South Africa)
Camera	Nikon F3
Lens	400 mm
Film	Tri–X

68

Title	'Barbra'
Photographer	John Davidson (UK)
Camera	Nikon F2
Lens	300 mm
Film	Tri–X

69

Title	'Ronnie Corbett'
Photographer	John Davidson (UK)
Camera	Nikon F2
Lens	180 mm
Film	Tri–X

70

Title	'Foot'
Photographer	Bernard Lequint (UK)
Camera	Leica M3
Lens	90 mm
Film	Plus–X

71

Title	'The Meeting'
Photographer	David Chamberlain ARPS (UK)
Camera	Mamiya
Lens	90 mm
Film	FP 4

72

Title	'Some Ride, Some Walk'
Photographer	Chas Thompson (UK)
Camera	Rolleiflex SL 35
Lens	85 mm
Film	HP 5

73

Title	'Magic Water'
Photographer	Manuel Monjibar Cortes (Spain)
Camera	Pentax F
Lens	150 mm
Film	Tri–X

74

Title	'Little Bunny'
Photographer	Ian Spratt (UK)
Camera	Nikon FE
Lens	135 mm Nikkor
Film	HP 5

75 Upper

Title	'Easel Fun'
Photographer	Ian Spratt (UK)
Camera	Nikon FE
Lens	135 mm Nikkor
Film	HP 5

75 Lower
Title	'OH!'
Photographer	Ian Spratt (UK)
Camera	Nikon FE
Lens	135 mm Nikkon
Film	HP 5

76
Title	'Winter Network'
Photographer	Derek J. Grant ARPS (UK)
Camera	Canon AE1
Lens	24 mm
Film	FP 4

77
Title	'A Tree In The Way!'
Photographer	Ludwig Schlinkmann (West Germany)
Camera	Mamiya 6 x 6
Lens	80 mm
Film	Tech. data not supplied

78
Photographer	Andrzej Krynicki (Poland)
Camera	Pentax 6 x 7
Lens	35 mm Fisheye
Film	Orwo NP 27

79
Photographer	Stanislaw Trzaska (Poland)
Camera	Nikon F2
Lens	24 mm
Film	Tri–X

80
Title	'Diane'
Photographer	John Russel (UK)
Camera	Nikon FE
Lens	24 mm
Film	HP 5

81
Title	'Red'
Photographer	Antonio Bonet Rius (Spain)
Camera	Nikon FE
Lens	135 mm Nikkor
Film	Kodachrome 64

82
Title	'La Belle Madame'
Photographer	Ron Smith (UK)
Camera	Praktica LTL
Lens	Tech. Data Not Supplied
Film	Orwell

83
Title	'Der Pfiefenraucher'
Photographer	Max Hess (Switzerland)
Camera	Pentax Spotmatic
Lens	Takumar 85 mm
Film	Kodachrome 25

84 Upper
Photographer	Manfred Kriegelstein (West Germany)
Camera	
Lens	Tech. data not supplied
Film	

84 Lower
Photographer	Manfred Kriegelstein (West Germany)
Camera	
Lens	Tech. data not supplied
Film	

85
Photographer	Michel Célérier (France)
Camera	Bronica S2 A 6 x 6
Lens	Tech. data not supplied
Film	Ektachrome 64. (Cibachrome)

86/87
Title	'Overflow'
Photographer	P Jeffery (UK)
Camera	Yashica FR
Lens	15 mm Yashica Fisheye
Film	Kodachrome 25

88
Title	'Les Ballons'
Photographer	Serge Guiolet (France)
Camera	Minolta XGl
Lens	28 mm
Film	Fujichrome

89
Photographer	Erik Steen (Norway)
Camera	Nikon F2
Lens	20 mm Nikkor wide angle
Film	Orwo UT 18

90
Title	'Night Train'
Photographer	Gerd Stieber (West Germany)
Camera	Pentax MX
Lens	135 mm
Film	Ektachrome 64

91 Upper
Title	'Poplar'
Photographer	Gerd Stieber (West Germany)
Camera	Pentax MX
Lens	90 mm
Film	Ektachrome 64

91 Lower
Title	'Autumn'
Photographer	Gerd Stieber (West Germany)
Camera	Pentax MX
Lens	200 mm
Film	Ektachrome 64

92
Title	'After Ski Race'
Photographer	Erikki Niemelä (Finland)
Camera	Leica M5
Lens	Elmarit 135 mm
Film	Kodachrome 25

93
Title	'Horse Racing on Ice'
Photographer	Steve Powell (UK)
Camera	Nikon F2
Lens	600 mm F4
Film	Kodachrome 64

94 Upper
Title	'RAF Red Arrows'
Photographer	David Higgs (UK)
Camera	Olympus OM2N
Lens	16 mm
Film	Ektachrome 64

94 Lower
Title	U.S. Nuclear Decontamination Exercise
Photographer	David Higgs (UK)
Camera	Olympus OM2N
Lens	Zuiko 24 mm
Film	Ektachrome 64

95 Upper
Photographer	Norman Pealing (UK)
Camera	Hasselblad 500 c/m
Lens	Tech. data not supplied
Film	Vericolor Negative

95 Lower
Title	'Bristol Returning from Falklands'
Photographer	R Moseley (UK)
Camera	Bronica SZA
Lens	50 mm
Film	Agfa 80S medium speed

96
Photographer	Margotte Magnus (UK)
Camera	Pentax 6 x 7
Lens	105 mm
Film	Ektachrome 160

97
Title	'Friends'
Photographer	Naresh Sohal (UK)
Camera	Olympus OM 2N
Lens	50 mm Zuiko
Film	FP 4

98
Title	'House at Crossroads Near Salzburg'
Photographer	Mike Taylor (UK)
Camera	Canon A1
Lens	70/210 mm zoom
Film	FP 4

99
Photographer	Vlado Bača (Czechoslovakia)
Camera	Mamiya 6 x 7
Lens	250 mm
Film	Orwo NP 20

100
Photographer	Vlado Bača (Czechoslovakia)
Camera	Pentax Spotmatic
Lens	50 mm
Film	Agfa 150 Pan

101
Photographer	Vlado Bača (Czechoslovakia)
Camera	Pentax Spotmatic
Lens	50 mm
Film	Agfa 150 Pan

102/103
Title	'Baloon Over Longleat'
Photographer	Ian Spratt (UK)
Camera	Nikon FE
Lens	35 mm Nikkor
Film	Tri–X

104
Title	'The Door'
Photographer	Josep Maria Ribas I Prous (Spain)
Camera	Nikon F
Lens	20 mm
Film	Tri–X

105
Photographer	Max Fund (Argentina)
Camera	Pentax SP
Lens	35mm
Film	HP 5

106
Title	'We Are Amused'
Photographer	Howard Walker (UK)
Camera	Nikon F3
Lens	300 mm
Film	HP 5

107
Title	'Smiling Princess'
Photographer	Stephen Shakeshaft (UK)
Camera	Nikon
Lens	85 mm
Film	Tech. data not supplied

108
Title	'Felucca On The Nile, Egypt'
Photographer	Jenifer Roberts ARPS (UK)
Camera	Olympus OM1
Lens	135 mm Zuiko
Film	FP 4

109
Title	'Boats At Kumbh Mela'
Photographer	S Paul (India)
Camera	
Lens	Tech. data not supplied
Film	

110
Title	'Picnic'
Photographer	Manfred Fitzner (West Germany)
Camera	Minolta – XD – 5
Lens	135 mm
Film	Agfa Pan 100

111 Upper
Photographer	Peter Langovits (Estonia – U.S.S.R.)
Camera	
Lens	Tech. data not supplied
Film	

111 Lower
Photographer	Tony Ward (UK)
Camera	Canon FTB
Lens	17 mm
Film	Tech. data not supplied

112
Title	'African Beauty'
Photographer	Hector Zampaglione (Spain)
Camera	Leicaflex
Lens	Tech Data Not Supplied
Film	Tri–X

113

Photographer	Hector Zampaglione (Spain)
Camera	Leicaflex
Lens	Tech Data Not Supplied
Film	Tri–X

114

Title	'The Human Heart'
Photographer	Kevin Fitzpatrick (UK)
Camera	Pentax
Lens	55 mm
Film	FP4

This photograph shows an unusual view of the human heart with its blood vessels (Coronary Arteries and Viens) in position as they are in life. The blood vessels have been injected with coloured gelatin to facilitate their identification. The heart was treated chemically to render its surface transparent and finally photographed under fluid. A negative image was produced which illustrated the anatomical features more clearly.

Vue extraordinaire du coeur humain, avec ses vaisseaux sanguins (Artères et Veines Coronaires) en position réelle. Ces vaisseaux ont fait l'objet d'une injection de gélatine colorée pour faciliter leur identification. Le coeur a été traité pour rendre sa surface transparente, et, enfin, il a été photographié sous fluide. Il a été realisé une image négative pour accuser plus nettement les traits anatomiques.

Diese Aufnahme zeigt eine ungewöhnliche Ansicht des menschlichen Herzens mit den Blutgefäßen (Kranzarterien und Herzvenen) in der gleichen Lage wie im Leben. Die Blutgefäße wurden mit farbiger Gelatine injeziert, um sie besser erkennen zu können. Das Herz wurde chemisch behandelt, um die Oberfläche durchsichtig zu machen, und zum Schluß in einer Flüssigkeit fotografiert. Eine negative Abbildung wurde erzeugt, um die anatomischen Eigenschaften klarer aufzuzeigen.

En esta fotografía se aprecia una vista inusitada del corazón humano, con sus vasos sanguíeos (venas y arteries coronarias) posicionados como en vida. A los vasos sanguíneos se les ha inyectado una gelatina coloreada para facilitar su identificación. El corazón fue tratado químicamente con el fin de dar transparencia a su superficie, y finalment se fotografió en un medio líquido. Se obtuvo una imagen negativa que ilustra las características anatómicas con mayor claridad.

115

Title	'Winter Near Heidelberg'
Photographer	Hans-Ulrich Comberg (West Germany)
Camera	Leica SL2
Lens	Macro-Elmarit-R
Film	Ilford Pan F

116

Title	'Football Ballet'
Photographer	Bodo Goeke (West Germany)
Camera	Canon A1
Lens	85 mm
Film	Tech. data not supplied

117

Title	'Feeling The Pinch'
Photographer	James Meehan (Eire)
Camera	Nikon F3
Lens	300 mm
Film	HP 5

118

Title	'If You Want To Know The Time'
Photographer	Mike Hollist (UK)
Camera	Nikon F2
Lens	105 mm
Film	Tri–X

119

Title	'Twin Police Cadets Passing Out'
Photographer	Eddie Brown (UK)
Camera	Nikon F2
Lens	85 mm
Film	Tri–X

120/121

Photographer	Branko Težak (Yugoslavia)
Camera	
Lens	Tech. data not supplied
Film	

122

Title	'Study In Stripes'
Photographer	Horst Friedrichs (West Germany)
Camera	Nikon FE
Lens	50 mm
Film	Tri–X

123

Title	'Contours'
Photographer	Ian Jebbett ARPS (UK)
Camera	Nikon F3
Lens	105 mm
Film	Ilford – XPI

124

Title	'Girl Watching A Punch & Judy Show'
Photographer	Clive B Harrison FRPS (UK)
Camera	Olympus OMI
Lens	100 mm
Film	XPI – 400

125

Title	'Three's A Crowd'
Photographer	S Riley LRPS (UK)
Camera	Mamiya C33
Lens	80 mm
Film	FP 4

125

Title	'Children At Play In Widnes Park'
Photographer	S. Riley LRPS (UK)
Camera	Mamiya
Lens	80 mm
Film	FP 4

126

Title	'Mountain Peak'
Photographer	Giuseppe Balla (Italy)
Camera	Canon F1
Lens	50 mm
Film	FP 4

127 Upper

Title	'Towards The Summit'
Photographer	Giuseppe Balla (Italy)
Camera	Canon F1
Lens	50 mm
Film	Tri–X

127 Lower

Title	'Storm at 4000 metres'
Photographer	Giuseppe Balla (Italy)
Camera	Canon F1
Lens	200 mm
Film	FP 4

128 Upper

Title	'Workers Sheltering From The Rain At An Oil Refinery In Mexico'
Photographer	Steve Benbow (UK)
Camera	Olympus OM2
Lens	100 mm
Film	Tri–X

128 Lower

Title	'Slow Shutter In The Paris Metro'
Photographer	R. Neathey (UK)
Camera	Olympus OM2
Lens	Tech. data not supplied
Film	FP 4

129

Title	'Ballooning In Alaska'
Photographer	Bruce Lloyd (UK)
Camera	Olympus OM2
Lens	Zuiko 75–150 mm zoom
Film	Tech. data not supplied

130

Title	'Jet Stream.' (Sodium Hiosulphate, Hypo Crystal X50 Polarised light)
Photographer	C. J. Kocher (UK)
Camera	
Lens	Tech. data not supplied
Film	

131

Title	'Parnell Square Dublin'
Photographer	Daniel Chenu (UK)
Camera	Nikon F2 AS
Lens	Nikkor 35 mm
Film	Kodacolor 400

132

Photographer	Jorge Lewinski (UK)
Camera	Pentax 6 x 7
Lens	55 mm
Film	Agfachrome 50S

133

Photographer	Jorge Lewinski (UK)
Camera	Pentax 6 x 7
Lens	55 mm
Film	Agfachrome 50S

134

Title	'Wilmslow Mini Rugby'
Photographer	Mike Brett (UK)
Camera	Nikon F2
Lens	200 mm
Film	Ektachrome 400

135

Title	'The Height Of Ambition'
Photographer	A Wharton (UK)
Camera	Pentax Spotmatic
Lens	135 mm Super Takuma
Film	Kodachrome

136/137

Title	'Sailing By'
Photographer	Peter M Rees (UK)
Camera	Olympus OMI N
Lens	Tamron 70–150mm zoom
Film	Kodachrome 64

138

Title	'Elvin Jones at Bracknell Jazz Festival'
Photographer	Christian Him (UK)
Camera	Olympus OM 2n
Lens	200 mm Zuiko
Film	Tech. data not supplied

139

Title	'The African Drum Ensemble at The Camden Jazz Festival'
Photographer	Christian Him (UK)
Camera	Olympus OM 2n
Lens	24 mm Zuiko
Film	Tech. data not supplied

140 Upper

Title	'Horned Lizard Eating A House Cricket'
Photographer	Pat Clay (UK)
Camera	Nikon FE
Lens	105 mm Micro Nikkor
Film	Kodachrome 25

140 Lower

Title	'Robin Moth – Showing Feathered Antennae'
Photographer	Pat Clay (UK)
Camera	Nikon FE
Lens	55 mm Micro Nikkor
Film	Kodachrome 25

141 Upper

Title	'South African Bull Frog'
Photographer	Heather Angel (UK)
Camera	Hasselblad 500 c/m
Lens	80 mm & Extension Tubes
Film	Kodachrome 64

141 Lower

Title	'Painted Reed Frog – Calling At Night'
Photographer	Heather Angel (UK)
Camera	Nikon F2
Lens	105 mm Micro – Nikkor
Film	Kodachrome 64

142

Title	'Start of Piccadilly Marathon at Manchester University'
Photographer	Mike Brett (UK)
Camera	Canon A1
Lens	50 mm
Film	Ektachrome 200

143
Photographer	T Green (UK)
Camera	Pentax SP 1000
Lens	Tech. data not supplied
Film	Ektachrome 200

144 Upper
Title	'Hong Kong Detail'
Photographer	Robert Hallman (UK)
Camera	Kowa Super 66
Lens	150 mm
Film	Agfa 50S

144 Lower
Title	'Candido Erotico'
Photographer	J W Legate (UK)
Camera	Pentax Spotmatic 1000
Lens	135 mm
Film	Kodachrome 64

145
Title	'Lake Siesta, Yosemite National Park'
Photographer	Bob Gray (UK)
Camera	Nagaoka 5 x 4
Lens	210 mm
Film	FP 4

146
Title	Wally Levis of Australia tackles a Great Britain player in the Rugby League Test at Wigam
Photographer	Mike Brett (UK)
Camera	Nikon
Lens	300 mm
Film	HP 5

147
Title	'Going Up'
Photographer	Mike Brett (UK)
Camera	Nikon
Lens	300 mm
Film	FP 5

148
Title	'Orphan Of The World' A refugee from Afghanistan
Photographer	Mike Hollist (UK)
Camera	Nikon F2
Lens	180 mm
Film	Tri–X

149 Upper
Photographer	Dennis Mansell AIIP, ARPS (UK)
Camera	Pentax
Lens	55 mm
Film	Tri–X

150/151
Title	'Water Seller In Marrakesh'
Photographer	Walter Schollmayer (West Germany)
Camera	Nikon FM2
Lens	105 mm
Film	FP 4

152
Title	'The Premiers Surprise'
Photographer	Mike Hollist (UK)
Camera	Nikon F2
Lens	105 mm
Film	Tri–X

153
Title	'Ted Heath Listening To Margaret Thatcher At Party Conference'
Photographer	A Markey (UK)
Camera	Nikon F2
Lens	Tech. data not supplied
Film	HP 5

154 Upper
Photographer	Bill Wisden FRPS (UK)
Camera	Pentax
Lens	16 mm
Film	Tech. data not supplied

154 Lower
Photographer	Bill Wisden FRPS (UK)
Camera	Pentax
Lens	20 mm
Film	Tech. data not supplied

155
Title	'Holiday Homes'
Photographer	William Cheung FRPS (UK)
Camera	Olympus OM2
Lens	300 mm
Film	FP 4

156
Title	'Gymnasts At The Dynamo Club In Moscow'
Photographer	Josep Maria Ribas I Prous (Spain)
Camera	Nikon F
Lens	105 mm
Film	Tri–X

157
Photographer	Oldřich Karásek (Czechoslovakia)
Camera	
Lens	Tech. data not supplied
Film	

158/159
Title	'Indian Station'
Photographer	David Burrows (UK)
Camera	
Lens	Tech. data not supplied
Film	

160
Title	'Pelican'
Photographer	W. O. Turnbull LRPS (UK)
Camera	Leicaflex SL2
Lens	135 mm Elmarit–R
Film	FP 4

161
Title	Actor Peter O'Toole
Photographer	Denis Thorpe (UK)
Camera	Leica M2
Lens	Summicron 50 mm
Film	HP5

162

Title	'Nude Behind Door'
Photographer	David Chamberlain ARPS (UK)
Camera	Contax RTS
Lens	85 mm
Film	HP 5

163

Title	'Low Light'
Photographer	David Chamberlain ARPS (UK)
Camera	Contax RTS
Lens	35 mm
Film	HP 5

164

Title	Sikhander Bakht Pakistan's medium pace bowler in action against the minor counties
Photographer	Gary Browne (UK)
Camera	Canon F1
Lens	Tech. data not supplied
Film	HP5

165

Title	'Vitamins Plus'
Photographer	Oleg Homola (Czechoslovakia)
Camera	
Lens	Tech. data not supplied
Film	

166

Title	'Supermog'
Photographer	T.S.Norton (UK)
Camera	Hasselblad
Lens	80 mm
Film	Tri–X

167

Title	'A Town Bird'
Photographer	Oleg Homola (Czechoslovakia)
Camera	
Lens	Tech. data not supplied
Film	

168

Title	'Onlooker At Speakers Corner'
Photographer	Neale Davison ARPS (UK)
Camera	Pentax SPII
Lens	200 mm
Film	Tri–X

169

Title	'Argument At Speakers Corner'
Photographer	Neale Davison ARPS (UK)
Camera	Pentax SPII
Lens	55 mm
Film	Tri–X

170

Title	'Down In The World'
Photographer	Tracey Chamberlain (UK)
Camera	Canon AE1
Lens	150 mm
Film	HP 5

171

Title	'So Unladylike'
Photograper	Keith Brown FRPS (UK)
Camera	Minolta
Lens	135 mm
Film	FP 4

172/173

Title	'Philipp'
Photographer	Karl Ziegler (West Germany)
Camera	Nikon F2
Lens	35 mm
Film	Ilford Pan F

174

Photographer	Christian Vogt (Switzerland)
Camera	
Lens	Tech. data not supplied
Film	

175

Title	'Bare Back'
Photographer	Benito Moya Vivar (Spain)
Camera	Nikon F
Lens	28 mm
Film	Tri–X

176

Title	'Olympic Gymnast Suzanne Dando
Photographer	Tony Ward (UK)
Camera	Canon A1
Lens	135 mm
Film	Tech. data not supplied

177

Title	'Reisanbau'
Photographer	Dieter Neumann (West Germany)
Camera	Nikon FE
Lens	80–200 mm zoom
Film	Agfa 50S

178

Title	'The Picnic'
Photographer	Walter Jones (UK)
Camera	Canon A1
Lens	50 mm
Film	Kodachrome 64

179 Upper

Title	'Le Mans 24hr Race'
Photographer	W. H. Murenbeeld (UK)
Camera	Canon F1
Lens	7.5 mm 180 Fisheye Canon F1
Film	Ektachrome 64

179 Lower

Title	'Getaway Car'
Photographer	Derek J Grant (UK)
Camera	Canon AE1
Lens	24 mm wide angle lens
Film	Ilford FP4 200

180
Photographer P I Foord
(West Germany)
Camera Linhof Kardan Super Color
Lens Tech. data not supplied
Film Ektachrome 64

181
Photographer F Karikese (Belgium)
Camera Nikkormat EL
Lens Nikkor 24 mm
Film Ektachrome 64

182/183
Title 'Berg Kirchl (in the
Villnöss—Valley Tyrol North
Italy)
Photographer Dieter Neumann
(West Germany)
Camera Nikon FE
Lens 80—200 mm zoom
Film Ektachrome 64

184
Photographer Pedro Luis Raota
(Argentina)
Camera
Lens Tech. data not supplied
Film

185
Photographer Pedro Luis Raota
(Argentina)
Camera
Lens Tech. data not supplied
Film

186
Photographer N. G. Patel (UK)
Camera Canon A1
Lens 70—71 mm zoom
Film Ektachrome 64

187
Title 'A Blackpool Model'
Photographer Peter W Tryuk (UK)
Camera Canon A1
Lens 70—210mm Canon Zoom
Film High Speed Ektachrome

188
Title 'Herst'
Photographer Sandor Rozsa's
(Switzerland)
Camera
Lens Tech. data not supplied
Film

189
Title 'Circles'
Photographer R. M. Johnson (UK)
Camera Pentax K1000 SLR
Lens Tech. data not supplied
Film Kodachrome 64

190
Title 'Start'
Photograper Veikko Wallström
(Finland)
Camera Nikon FTN
Lens Nikkor zoom 43-86 mm
Film Ektachrome 64

191
Title 'Pursuit'
Photographer Veikko Wallström
(Finland)
Camera Nikon FTN
Lens Nikkor zoom 43-86mm
Film Ektachrome 64

192 Upper
Title 'South Bishop Lighthouse'
Photographer Jacki Sime (UK)
Camera Nikon
Lens Nikkor
Film Kodachrome 64

192 Lower
Photographer D Whiteoak
Camera Canon AV1
Lens Standard 50 mm
Film Agfa CT 21

193
Photographer Stephen Shakeshaft (UK)
Camera Nikon
Lens 28 mm
Film Tech. data not supplied

194
Photographer Antanas Sutkus AFIAP
(Lithuania — USSR)
Camera Hasselblad
Lens Tech. data not supplied
Film Tech. data not supplied

195
Title 'Don't Be Afraid'
Photograper Leona Korkutiene
(Lithuania — USSR)
Camera
Lens Tech. data not supplied
Film

196/197
Title Injured P.C John Davies
reunited with his injured
mount 'Echo'
Photographer Mike Hollist (UK)
Camera Nikon F2
Lens 180 mm
Film Tri—X

198
Title 'Kitten At Barn Door'
Photographer Jane Miller ARPS (UK)
Camera Mamiya
Lens 80 mm
Film Tri—X

199
Title 'Bruin'
Photographer Ian E Rodger (UK)
Camera Nikon FM
Lens 85 mm
Film HP 5

200
Title 'Accident'
Photographer Veikko Wallström ARPS
(Finland)
Camera Nikon FE
Lens 200 M
Film Tri—X

201
Title 'Washday'
Photographer Veikko Wallström ARPS (Finland)
Camera Nikon FT
Lens Zoom
Film Tri–X

202
Title 'Icarus'
Photograper Arnold Umlauf EFIAP (West Germany)
Camera Canon A.1
Lens Tech. data not supplied
Film FP 4

203
Photographer Asadour Guzelian (UK)
Camera Pentax
Lens 200 mm
Film Tri–X

204/205
Title 'Belfast's First Marathon'
Photographer Stanley Matchett (UK)
Camera Nikon F2
Lens 300 mm
Film HP 5

206
Title 'Sara'
Photographer Giuseppe Balla (Italy)
Camera Canon F1
Lens 100 mm
Film HP 5

207
Title
Photographer Felipe Iguiñiz (Spain)
Camera Hasselblad
Lens 150 mm
Film Tri–X

208
Title 'Thirsty Weekend Near Prague'
Photographer Fantišek Dostál (Czechoslovakia)
Camera Minolta
Lens 35 mm
Film Orwo NP 20

209
Title 'Watch Your Step'
Photograper Martin J O'Neill (UK)
Camera Nikon FM
Lens 105 mm
Film Tri–X

210
Photographer Hansjochen Heinecke (West Germany)
Camera
Lens Tech. data not supplied
Film

211
Photographer Hansjochen Heinecke (West Germany)
Camera
Lens Tech. data not supplied
Film

212
Title 'Winter Ride In A Small Village In Austria'
Photographer Manfred Gsteu AFIAP (Austria)
Camera Minolta
Lens 135 mm
Film HP 5

213 Upper
Title Farmers setting out to look for trapped sheep on the South Downs
Photographer Colin Westgate FRPS (UK)
Camera Konica
Lens 100 mm
Film FP 4

213 (Lower)
Title 'Winter Near Heidelberg'
Photographer Hans–Ulrich Comberg (West Germany)
Camera Leicaflex SL 2
Lens Macro–Elmarit–R
Film Ilford Pan F

214
Title 'The Preacher'
Photograper Richard Summersby (UK)
Camera Pentax
Lens 105 mm
Film FP 4

215
Title 'Onlookers at Speakers Corner'
Photographer Neale Davison ARPS (UK)
Camera Pentax
Lens 200 mm
Film Tri-X

216/217
Title 'Paris Magazine Seller'
Photographer Howard Walker (UK)
Camera Leica M4
Lens 35 mm
Film HP 5

218
Title 'Jochen And Andrea'
Photographer Karl Ziegler (West Germany)
Camera Nikon F2
Lens 35 mm
Film Ilford Pan F

219
Title 'Match'
Photographer Karl Ziegler (West Germany)
Camera Nikon F2
Lens 35 mm
Film Ilford Pan F

220/221
Title 'Party–Goers at a May Ball at Harewood House Yorkshire'
Photographer Asadour Guzelian (UK)
Camera Pentax
Lens 24 mm
Film Tri–X

222 Upper

Photographer Ole Sand (Denmark)
Camera Nikkormat FT 2
Lens 50 mm
Film Tri–X

222 Lower

Photograper Jagdish Agarwal (India)
Camera Nikon F2
Lens Tech. data not supplied
Film Orwo

223

Photographer (From Russia)
Camera
Lens Tech. data not supplied
Film

224

Title 'Don't Take My Mummy's Picture'
Photographer R.A. Acharya (India)
Camera Pentax Spotmatic
Lens 50 mm
Film Orwo NP 55

225

Title 'Summer'
Photographer Romnaldas Požerskis (Lithuania U.S.S.R)
Camera Minolta XDII
Lens 28 mm Rokkor
Film Orwo KN–3

226

Title 'The Sword Of Damocles'
Photographer Antonio Grau i Lopez (Spain)
Camera
Lens Tech. data not supplied
Film

Rear End Paper

Title 'Tyrolean Landscape'
Photographer Denis Thorpe (UK)
Camera Nikon F2
Lens 200 mm
Film FP 4